MEASURE FOR MEASURE

By WILLIAM SHAKESPEARE

Preface and Annotations by
HENRY N. HUDSON

Introduction by
CHARLES HAROLD HERFORD

Measure for Measure
By William Shakespeare
Preface and Annotations by Henry N. Hudson
Introduction by Charles Harold Herford

Print ISBN 13: 978-1-4209-5837-9
eBook ISBN 13: 978-1-4209-5838-6

Cover Image: a detail of "Mariana" by V. C. Prinser, from "The graphic gallery of Shakespeare's heroines", Sampson Low, Marston & Co., Ltd., London, c. 1896.

Please visit *www.digireads.com*

CONTENTS

Preface

First printed in the folio of 1623; and no other authentic contemporary notice of it has reached us. The strongly-marked peculiarities of the piece in language, cast of thought, and moral temper, have invested it with great psychological interest, and bred a special desire among critics to connect it in some way with the author's mental history,—with some supposed crisis in his feelings and experience. Hence the probable date of the writing was for a long time argued more strenuously than the subject would otherwise seem to justify; and, as often falls out in such cases, the more the critics argued the point, the further they were from coming to an agreement. And, in truth, the plain matter-of-fact critics have here succeeded much better in the work than their more philosophical brethren; which aptly shows how little the brightest speculation can do in questions properly falling within the domain of facts.

In default of other data, the critics in question based their arguments upon certain probable allusions to contemporary matters; especially on those passages which express the Duke's fondness for "the life removed," and his aversion to being greeted by crowds of people. Chalmers brought forward also the very pertinent fact of a long-sleeping statute having been revived in 1604, which punished with death all divorced or divorcing persons who married again while their former husbands or wives were living. This circumstance, he thinks, might well have suggested what is said by the Duke:

> We have strict statutes and most biting laws,—
> The needful bits and curbs to headstrong steeds,—
> Which for this fourteen years we have let sleep;
> Even like an o'ergrown lion in a cave,
> That goes not out to prey.

Chalmers had the sagacity to discover also a sort of portrait-like resemblance in the Duke to King James the First. As the King was indeed a much better theologian than statesman or ruler, the fact of the Duke's appearing rather more at home in the cowl and hood than in his ducal robes certainly lends some colour to this discovery.

The King's unamiable repugnance to being gazed upon by throngs of admiring subjects is thus spoken of by a contemporary writer: "In his public appearance, especially in his sports, the accesses of the people made him so impatient, that he often dispersed them with frowns, that we may not say, with curses." And his churlish bearing towards the crowds which, prompted by eager loyalty, flocked forth to hail his accession, is noted by several historians. But he was a pretty free encourager of the Drama, as well as of other liberal preparations; and, with those who had tasted, or who sought, his patronage, it was natural that these symptoms of weakness should pass for tokens of a wise superiority to the dainties of popular applause. All which renders it not unlikely that the Poet may have had an eye to the King in the passages cited by Malone in support of his conjecture:

> I love the people,
> But do not like to stage me to their eyes:
> Though it do well, I do not relish well
> Their loud applause and aves vehement;
> Nor do I think the man of safe discretion
> That does affect it.
> So play the foolish throngs with one that swoons;
> Come all to help him, and so stop the air
> By which he should revive: and even so
> The general, subject to a well-wish'd king,
> Quit their own part, and in obsequious fondness
> Crowd to his presence, where their untaught love
> Must needs appear offence.

The allusion here being granted, Malone's inference, that the play was made soon after the King's accession, and before the effect of his unlooked-for austerity on this score had spent itself, was natural enough. Nor is the conjecture of Ulrici and others without weight, "that Shakespeare was led to the composition of the play by the rigoristic sentiments and arrogant virtue of the Puritans." And in this view several points of the main action might have been aptly suggested at the time in question: for the King had scarcely set foot in England but he began to be worried by the importunities of that remarkable people; who had been feeding upon the hope, that by the sole exercise of his prerogative he would work through a radical change in the constitution of the Church, and so bring her into accordance with their ideas: all this on the principle, of course, that a minority however small, with the truth, was better than a majority however large, without it.

The accession of King James to the English throne was in March, 1603. So that the forecited arguments would conclude the writing of the play to have been nearly synchronous with the revisal of *All's Well*, and with the production of *King Lear*; at least, within the same period of three or four years. The characteristics of style and temper draw to the same conclusion as regards the date of the writing.

There is no doubt that for some particulars in the plot and story of *Measure for Measure* the Poet was ultimately indebted to Cinthio, an Italian novelist of the sixteenth century. The original story makes the eighty-fifth in his *Hundred Tales*. A youth named Ludovico is there overtaken in the crime of seduction: Juriste, a magistrate highly reputed for wisdom and justice, passes sentence of death upon him; and Ludovico's sister, a virgin of rare gifts and graces, goes to pleading for his life. Her beauty and eloquence have the same effect on Juriste as Isabella's on Angelo. His proposals are rejected with scorn and horror; but the lady, overcome by the pathetic entreaties of her brother, at last yields to them under a solemn promise of marriage. His object being gained, the wicked man then commits a double vow-breach, neither marrying the sister nor sparing the brother. She appeals to the Emperor, by whom Juriste is forced to marry her, and then sentenced to death; but is finally pardoned at the lady's suit, who is now as earnest and eloquent for her husband as she had been for her brother. Her conduct touches him with remorse, and at length proves as effective in reforming his character as it was in redeeming his life.

As early as 1578, this tale was dramatized after a sort by George Whetstone, and was published as *The History of Promos and Cassandra*. Whetstone was a writer of learning and talent, but not such that even the instructions of Shakespeare could have made him capable of dramatic excellence; and, as he had no such benefit, his performance is insipid and worthless enough. The drama is in Two Parts, and is written in verse, with alternate rhymes. In his conduct of the story Whetstone varies somewhat from the original; as the following abstract will show:

In the city of Julio, then under the rule of Corvinus, King of Hungary, there was a law that for incontinence the man should suffer death, and the woman be marked out for infamy by her dress. Through the indulgence of magistrates, this law came to be little regarded. The government falling at length into the hands of Lord Promos, he revived the statute, and, a youth named Andrugio being convicted of the fault in question, resolved to visit the penalties in their utmost rigour upon both the parties. Andrugio had a sister of great virtue and accomplishment, named Cassandra, who undertook to sue for his life. Her good behaviour, great beauty, and "the sweet order of her talk" wrought so far with the governor as to induce a short reprieve. Being inflamed soon after with a criminal passion, he set down the spoil of her honour as the ransom. She spurned his suit with abhorrence. Unable, however, to resist the pleadings of her brother, she at last yielded to the man's proposal, on condition of his pardoning her brother and then marrying her. This he vowed to do; but, his end once gained, instead of keeping his vow, he ordered the jailer to present Cassandra with her brother's head. As the jailer knew what the governor had done, he took the head of a felon just executed, and set Andrugio at liberty. Cassandra, supposing the head to be her brother's, was at the point to kill herself for grief, but spared that stroke, to be avenged on the traitor. She devised to make her case known to the King; who forthwith hastened to do justice on Promos, ordering that, to repair the lady's honour, he should marry her, and then, for his crime against the State, lose his head. No sooner was Cassandra a wife than all her rhetoric of eye, tongue, and action was tasked to procure the pardon of her husband; but the King, tendering the public good more than hers, denied her suit. At length, Andrugio, overcome by his sister's grief, made himself known; for he had all the while been about the place in disguise; whereupon the King, to honour the virtues of Cassandra, pardoned both him and Promos.

In 1592, Whetstone published his *Heptameron of Civil Discourses*, containing a prose version of the same tale. It is observable that he deviates from Cinthio in bringing Andrugio off alive; and as Shakespeare does the same with Claudio, we may well conclude that he drew directly from Whetstone, not from the original author. Beyond the mere outline of the story, it does not appear that the Poet borrowed any thing more than a few slight hints and casual expressions. And a comparison of the two pieces would nowise reduce his claims; it being not less creditable to have lifted the story out of the mire into such a region of art and poetry than to have invented it. Then too, even as regards the story, Shakespeare varies from Whetstone much more materially than the latter does from Cinthio: representing the illicit meeting of Claudio and Juliet as taking place under the shield of a solemn betrothment; which very much lessens their fault, as marriage-bonds were already upon them; and proportionably heightens Angelo's wickedness, as it brings on him the guilt of making the law responsible for his own arbitrary rigour. But the main *original* feature in the plot of *Measure for Measure* is the part of Mariana, which puts a new life into the whole, and purifies it almost into another nature; as it prevents the soiling of Isabella's womanhood, supplies an apt reason for the Duke's mysterious conduct, and yields a pregnant motive for Angelo's pardon, in that his life is thereby bound up with that of a wronged and innocent woman, whom his crimes are made the occasion of restoring to her rights and happiness; so that her virtue may be justly allowed to reprieve him from death.

I have already referred to certain characteristics of style and temper which this play shares with several others probably written about the same time, and which, as before observed, have been thought to mark some crisis in the Poet's life. It cannot well be denied that the plays in question have something of a peculiar spirit, which might aptly suggest that some passage of bitter experience must have turned the milk of his genius for a time into gall, and put him upon a course of harsh and indignant thought. The point is well stated by Hallam: "There seems to have been a period of Shakespeare's life when his heart was ill at ease, and ill content with the world or his own conscience: the memory of hours misspent, the pang of affection misplaced or unrequited, the experience of man's worser nature, which intercourse with ill-chosen associates peculiarly teaches,—these, as they sank down into the depths of his great mind, seem not only to have inspired into it the conception of Lear and Timon, but that of one primary character, the censurer of mankind. This type is first seen in the philosophic melancholy of Jaques, gazing with an undiminished serenity, and with a gayety of fancy, though not of manners, on the follies of the world. It assumes a graver cast in the exiled Duke of the same play, and one rather more severe in the Duke of *Measure for Measure*? And Verplanck speaks in a similar strain of "that portion of the author's life which was memorable for the production of the additions to the original *Hamlet*, with their melancholy wisdom; probably of *Timon*, with its indignant and hearty scorn, and rebukes of the baseness of civilized society; and above all of *Lear*, with its dark pictures of unmixed, unmitigated guilt, and its terrible and prophet-like denunciations."

These words certainly carry much weight, and may go far to warrant the belief of the writers, that the Poet was smitten with some rude shock of fortune which untuned the melody of his soul, and wrenched his mind from its once smooth and happy course, causing it to recoil upon itself and brood over its own thoughts. Yet there are considerable difficulties besetting a theory of this kind. For, in some other plays referred by these critics to the same period, there is so much of the Poet's gayest and happiest workmanship as must greatly embarrass if not quite upset such a theory. But, whatever may have caused the peculiar tone and the cast of thought in the forenamed plays, it is pretty certain that the darkness was not permanent; the clear azure, soft sunshine, and serene sweetness of *The Tempest* and *The Winter's Tale* being unquestionably of a later date. And, surely, in the life of so earnest and thoughtful a man as Shakespeare, there might well be, nay, there must have been, times when, without any special woundings or bruisings of fortune, his mind got fascinated by the appalling mystery of evil that haunts our fallen nature.

That such darker hours, however occasioned, were more frequent at one period of the Poet's life than at others, is indeed probable. And it was equally natural that their coming should sometimes engage him in heart-tugging and brain-sweating efforts to scrutinize the inscrutable workings of human guilt, and thus stamp itself strongly upon the offspring of his mind. Thus, without any other than the ordinary progress of thoughtful spirits, we should naturally have a middle period, when the early enthusiasm of hope had passed away, and before the deeper, calmer, but not less cheerful tranquillity of resignation had set in. For so it is apt to be in this life of ours: the angry barkings of fortune, or what seem such, have their turn with us; "the fretful fever and the stir unprofitable " work our souls full of discord and perturbation; but after a while these things pass away, and are followed by a more placid and genial time; the experienced insufficiency of man for himself having charmed our wrestlings of thought into repose, and our spirits having undergone the chastening and subduing power of life's sterner discipline.

HENRY N. HUDSON.

1881.

Introduction

Measure for Measure was first published in the Folio of 1623, as the fourth in order of the Comedies. It was doubtless printed from the theatre-copy, and abounds in perplexed and corrupt passages, many of which no emendation has yet completely restored.

External evidence of the date of *Measure for Measure* is confined to a palpable reminiscence of certain lines of act ii. sc. 4, found in a poem of 1607. This was the *Myrrha* of W. Barksted, where these lines occur:

> And like as when some sudden extasie
>   Seizeth the nature of a sicklie man;
> When he's discerned to swoon, straight by and by
>   Folke to his help confusedly have ran,
> And seeking with their art to fetch him back,
>   So many throng, that he the ayre doth lacke.

An entry often quoted in the accounts of the Court *Revels*, mentioning a performance on 26th December 1604, is now known to be a forgery. But the date was well invented, for all indications point to 1603-4 as the year of its composition. Not to dwell upon possible allusions to the accession of James, noticed at i. 1. 68 and ii. 4. 27, the play is linked very closely both with *All's Well That Ends Well arid*, with *Hamlet*. And *Hamlet* was undoubtedly completed in 1602-3. The grave strenuousness of character which distinguishes Helena from the Rosalinds and Beatrices of the preceding group of Comedies is carried a step further in the passionate intensity of Isabel. In both, an immense inner force is normally concealed by a reserve not at all characteristic of Shakespearean womanhood; in both it breaks out at moments in splendours of poetry such as Portia alone among the women of the Comedies approaches. The device of Mariana is clearly adapted from the story of Helena. The affinities with *Hamlet* lie less in the characters than in the moral atmosphere.[1] Both plays are pervaded by an oppressive consciousness, new in Shakespeare, of the might of evil; the state of the world is something rotten, and those who would better it are paralysed by inner flaws of mind or will. Denmark is out of joint, and Vienna a sink of vice; the duke and Hamlet alike recognise, and alike seek to evade, the reformer's task. Hamlet groans and procrastinates; the duke quietly appoints a deputy, and the deputy, a saint among sinners, is made a sinner by a saint. In both Hamlet and the duke, it may be added, different critics have discovered resemblances to the bustling Solomon who had, perhaps, just taken his seat upon the English throne.

Measure for Measure closely follows in outline the plot of George Whetstone's *Promos and Cassandra*, published in 1578. The title of this performance is as follows: '*The right excellent and famous Historye | of | Promos and Cassandra*: | divided into two commical Discourses. | In the first Part is shewn, | The unsufferable Abuse of a lewd MAGISTRATE; | The vertuous Behaviours of a chaste LADYE; | The uncontrouled Lewdeness of a favoured CURTISAN: | And the undeserved estimation of a pernicious PARASYTE. | In the second part is discoursed, | The perfect magnanimity of a noble KING, | In checking Vice and favouring Vertue: | Wherein is shown | The Ruin and overthrow of dishonest practises: | With the advancement of upright dealings. The Work of George Whetstone, Gent.'

The Dedication, addressed to his kinsman, the Recorder of London, is one of the earliest Elizabethan manifestoes of dramatic principles we possess. He takes the whole contemporary drama, at home and abroad, vigorously to task. The Italian, French, and Spanish playwrights are too lascivious; the German 'too holy'; the English 'most vain, indiscreet, and out of order,' ignoring the limits of place and time, bringing 'Gods from Heaven and Devils from Hell,' and confusing the distinctions of character. 'Many times (to make mirth) they make a clown companion with a king; in their grave counsels they allow the advice of fools: yea, they use one order of speech for all persons.' In all these points Whetstone's 'work,' as he, like Jonson, characteristically called his play, for it was evidently the fruit of immense pains, exhibited an advance. The story, drawn from Cinthio's *Hecatommithi* (Dec. viii. Nov. 5) had the best characteristic of the Italian novel: a single, powerful motive, worked out within narrow

---

[1] Among many interesting detailed parallels we may note: Isabel's indictment of man 'dressed in authority,' and Hamlet's 'the insolence of office'; Claudio's and Hamlet's dread of the 'something after death.' And Isabel, like Hamlet, has to 'repel the insinuation that her righteous anger is the voice of madness' (v. 1. 50).

limits of place and time, and without any resort to marvel.[2] On the other hand, the characters were mere types, and the plot was handled with somewhat obtuse moral instinct. Whetstone made little advance in individuality of character; but his types—'the lewd Magistrate,' 'the chaste lady,' and the rest—are drawn with much rude vigour. Corvinus, king of Hungary, appoints Promos his deputy in the city of Julia, with a special charge 'to scoorge the wights, good Lawes that disobay.' Promos proceeds to revive the law against incontinence, upon which Andrugio (Claudio) is imprisoned. Andrugio appeals to his sister, Cassandra, who appeals to Promos to be merciful. The language of the scene is sufficiently rude, and in dramatic grip and nexus it breaks down altogether; but the germs of several Shakespearean motives are already discernible:—

[*She, kneeling, speaks to Promos.*]

Most mighty lord, and worthy judge, thy judgement sharp abate,
Vail thou thine ears to hear the plaint that wretched I relate,
Behold the woeful sister here of poor Andrugio,
Whom though that law awardeth death, yet mercy do him show:
Weigh his young years, the force of love, which forced his amiss,
Weigh, weigh that marriage works amends for what committed is.
He hath defiled no nuptial bed, nor forced rape hath moved;
He fell thro' love, who never meant but wive the wight he loved.

Prom. Cassandra, leave off thy bootless suit, by law he hath been
        tried,
        Law found his fault, law judged him death.
Cass. Yet this may be replied,
        That lawe a mischiefe oft permits, to keep due form of law,
        That lawe small faults, with greatest dooms, to keep men still
            in awe.
        Yet kings, or such as execute regal authoritie,

---

[2] Cinthio's novel seems to have been founded upon an actual occurrence of 1547, narrated in a letter from a Hungarian student in Vienna, Joseph Macarius, to a friend in Sárvár. Here the heroine undergoes dishonour in order to save her condemned husband, whose execution nevertheless proceeds, She appeals to the imperial governor of the province of Milan, who causes the judge to marry her, pay her 3000 ducats, and lose his head (translated in *Notes and Queries*, 29th July1893). This is probably the original of the story found in Goulart, *Histoires admirables et mémorables advenues de Nostre Temps*, 1607. Successive narrators softened one by one its tragic features. Cinthio saves the tyrannous judge from execution at the intercession of the lady; Whetstone similarly saves her condemned brother; Shakespeare finally saves the lady her self from dishonour. A more recent but not very convincing attempt has been made by Sarrazin to show that Shakespeare's duke, Vincentio, was modelled upon the contemporary duke of Mantua. Vincenzio Gonzaga (*Jahrbuch*, xxxi. 165).

If mends be made may overrule the force of lawe with mercie.
Here is no wylful murder wrought, which axeth blood againe;
Andrugio's fault may valued be, Marriage wipes out his
stayne.

Promos temporises, then, at a second interview, declares the price
of Andrugio's pardon. Cassandra proceeds to inform her brother, who
faces the alternatives like a practical man:

Here are two evils, the best hard to digest,
But where as things are driven unto necessity,
There are we byd, of both evils choose the least.
Cass. And of these evils, the least I hold is death.

But Andrugio urges the slander that she would incur by causing his
death; and moreover that Promos, having once experienced her love,
'no doubt but he to marriage will agree.' At this rather unfortunately
chosen moment Cassandra suddenly discovers that her honour is of less
account than her brother's life:

And shall I stick to stoupe to Promos' will
Since my brother enjoyeth life thereby? . . .
My Andrugio, take comfort in distresse,
Cassandra is wonne, thy raunsom great to paye,
Such care she hath, thy thraldom to release,
As she consentes her honor for to slay.

The 'ransom' is paid, but no reprieve arrives. This, however, is of
little moment, for Andrugio's gaoler, a man of sensitive conscience, has
released him, sending to Promos the head of one recently executed
instead of his. Cassandra seeks the king, tells her story, and, having told
it, draws a knife to end her dishonour in the manner of Lucrece. At the
king's entreaty she foregoes this resolve, and he prepares to call his
deputy to account. The second part opens with his approach. Promos
appears before him and is promptly condemned to lose his head, after
having first married Cassandra. But no sooner is the marriage ceremony
over than Cassandra exchanges the role of the wronged maiden for that
of the devoted wife, and implores his pardon. But the king is inflexible,
and Promos is already at the scaffold when the timely arrival of
Andrugio enables the king to remit the penalty 'for his wife's sake.'
To the reader of *Measure for Measure* all this seems intolerable
bungling. Whetstone himself evidently regarded his play with
complacency, for he reproduced the story, in Euphuistic prose, four
years later in his *Heptameron.* There he made an attempt to strengthen
the action at what was evidently its weakest point, the character of

Cassandra. But the task was far beyond his powers. He feels that the compliance of his 'chaste lady' with Promos' terms requires defence, but cannot decide whether to excuse it as a compulsory sin or to glorify it as a noble sacrifice. She is by turns Lucretia and Alcestis:

If this offence be known (quoth Andrugio) thy fame will bee enlarged, because it will likewise be known that thou receivedst dishonor to give thy brother life: if it be secret, thy conscience will be without scruple of guiltiness. Thus, known or unknown, thou shalt be deflow'red, but not dishonested, and for amends we both shall live.

Hereupon the narrator (Madam Isabella) interposes an appeal to her audience: 'Sovereign madam, and you fair gentlewomen, I intreat you in Cassandra's behalf, these reasons well weighed, to judge her yielding a constraint and no consent.' This 'judgment' is further enforced by an express reference to Lucretia, whose 'destiny' she seeks to emulate.

What arrested Shakespeare in this story was clearly the three great dramatic situations, here rudely outlined:—the sister pleading for her brother's life, the stern lawgiver violating his own law, and the brother pleading for his life at the cost of his sister's honour. Whetstone had spoiled two of these by making both Promos and Andrugio plead with success, and he had only contrived, by a series of violent suppositions, to bring the fortunes of brother and sister to a happy issue. So far as Claudio's deliverance is concerned, Shakespeare improves somewhat, but not very greatly, upon his original. Instead of the compassionate gaoler who simply lets his prisoner free, we have the provost—an admirable sketch of well-meaning but cautious and disciplined officialdom—who with difficulty consents merely to postpone · his execution. Instead of the head of an executed prisoner, the counterfeit of Claudio is derived from 'a pirate who died this morning of a cruel fever'—a change which saves the plot from an incongruous element of tragedy, but is otherwise of questionable merit. Cassandra's fate called for a more radical change. Such a fall as hers was absolutely repugnant to Shakespeare's art; at no period of his career would he have tolerated such an incident, on either of the hypotheses between which Whetstone so uneasily fluctuates. But the device by which Isabel's honour is saved cannot be acquitted of a certain poverty of invention: so supremely original a character as Isabel deserved a better fate than to play once more a played-out role from *All's Well*. The duke who wanders in disguise among his people and 'like power divine looks upon our passes,' has some advantages over Whetstone's absentee prince, but probability is not one of them; and his final distribution of rewards and punishments hardly affects to be plausible. Angelo's pardon and Isabel's marriage are concessions to the conventions of a comic *dénoûment*, lacking inner congruity with their character and antecedents, and scarcely true to the promise of the title.[3] Evidently, though Shakespeare meant to supply his company with a comedy, he treated the conventions of Comedy merely with an outer deference.

The determining animus of the wonderful transformation which he wrought in the story of Promos and Cassandra belongs to a wholly different order of ideas and experience. He had exhibited in *Twelfth Night* the comedy of an honest, *borne* man infatuated with self-esteem; in *Julius Cæsar*, the tragedy of a man of high but narrow principles rigidly applied to a complex situation; in *Hamlet*, the tragic paralysis of a noble will under the spell of a restless imaginative sensibility. It was an intellect charged with the ironic sense of the disasters which await the well-meaning in a world where only a passion for goodness can morally hold its own, that created the virtuous precisian Angelo out of the 'lewd tyrant' Promos, and the refined weakling Claudio out of the commonplace Andrugio; and that set over against both the sublime and unique figure of Isabel.

Angelo is best understood when approached from the side on which he is akin to Brutus. He is 'a precisian in power,' a man of austere principle, untried but perfectly sincere. But Brutus' simple and transparent nature forges its way through the drift of circumstances unchanged, provoking its own doom, but undergoing no moral collapse; while Angelo, after his first doctrinaire blunder, finds himself suddenly assailed at an unarmed point, and, with scarcely a thought, is ready to surrender the whole moral capital laid up in a blameless life as the price of the person of Isabel. The irony of his career is accentuated by the unseen presence at his elbow of the moral Mephistopheles who has armed him with power and who awaits the destined hour to call him to account. It is characteristic of the temper of the play that Shakespeare thus substituted for Whetstone's absentee ruler this incredible but effective Friar.

Claudio owes still more than Angelo to Shakespeare's refining art. He is relieved with exquisite delicacy against the hideous throng whose sin the law identifies with his. His first words of keen humiliation instantly distinguish him from the brazen Lucio. He has the virtues and the failings of the impulsive temperament. His imagination is as rich as Isabel's, but his will takes the colour of its changing visions. He cannot be said, like Angelo, to comply with or infringe a moral rule; he rather abandons himself to a stream of illuminated emotions, tending, as it may happen, to good or ill. Within a few sentences he is ready to 'encounter darkness as a bride,' and to shudder at the image of the 'cold obstruction' and the 'kneaded clod.' 'Conscience' makes a

---

[3] The title was probably suggested by the phrase 'Blood axeth blood' in Whetstone (ed. Hazlitt, p. 227).

coward of him,—a conscience inflamed with the vision of sensuous pleasures and pains.

Angelo and Claudio are failures in opposite schools of life; without much straining, we might say that they foreshadow the characteristic weaknesses of the Puritan and of the Cavalier. But, with whatever irony Shakespeare may have contemplated the pretensions of both ideals, so far as they were realised in his time, the character of Isabel assures us that a type of impassioned holiness such as inspired the finest embodiments of both, yet more akin on the whole to the austere and imperious holiness of Puritanism, appealed powerfully to Shakespeare when he wrote. In moral intensity, and also in her total absence of humour, she is rather Miltonic than Shakespearean—Miltonic in the gracious way of the lady in *Comus*, save that she has the higher grace of a chastity which she is ready to die for, but which it does not occur to her to celebrate. Her obvious affinities with Portia make the contrast more glaring. Like Portia, she intervenes to check legal crime; but Portia's plea for mercy cannot compare in ethical grip any more than in tragic intensity with hers. Portia's is an eloquent exposition of the beauty of well-doing; Isabel's is penetrated to the core with distrust of human nature, when armed with the demoralising engine of power. Put forth in the first years of the momentous seventeenth century, this great though dramatically unequal play is full of prophetic intimations: the scathing ridicule of tyrants may be put beside the courtly compliments, in the first scene, to a popular king. The temper of stern recognition of the heights and depths of good and evil pervades it; and through the web of ethical seriousness there runs a thread of that brooding intellectual curiosity apparent in the whole *Hamlet* period, the zest for probing the secrets of human nature, and finding 'what these seemers be'; for analysing character (whence the countless books of 'Characters' from Jonson's *Every Man out of His Humour* downwards); for beating at the gates of the unknown, and urging a charioted imagination to flights in the mystery beyond.

CHARLES HAROLD HERFORD.

1899.

MEASURE FOR MEASURE

DRAMATIS PERSONAE

VICENTIO, *Duke of Vienna.*
ANGELO, *Deputy in the Duke's absence.*
ESCALUS, *joined with Angelo in the Government.*
CLAUDIO.
LUCIO.
Provost of the Prison.
THOMAS, *Friar.*
PETER, *Friar.*
A Justice.
VARRIUS.
ELBOW, *a Constable.*
FROTH.
POMPEY, *a Clown, Servant to Mistress Overdone.*
ABHORSON, *an Executioner.*
BARNARDINE, *a dissolute Prisoner.*

ISABELLA, *Sister to Claudio.*
MARIANA, *betrothed to Angelo.*
JULIET, *beloved by Claudio.*
FRANCISCA, *a Nun.*
MISTRESS OVERDONE, *a Bawd.*

Lords, Officers, Citizens, Boy, and Attendants.

SCENE: *Vienna*

ACT I.

SCENE I.

An apartment in the DUKE'*s Palace.*

[*Enter* DUKE, ESCALUS, LORDS, *and* ATTENDANTS.]

DUKE. Escalus,—
ESCALUS. My lord.
DUKE. Of government the properties to unfold,
    Would seem in me t' affect speech and discourse;
    Since I am put to know[1] that your own science
    Exceeds, in that, the lists[2] of all advice
    My strength can give you: then no more remains
    But that to your sufficiency, as your worth is able,[3]
    And let them work. The nature of our people,
    Our city's institutions, and the terms
    For common justice, you are as pregnant[4] in
    As art and practice hath enriched any
    That we remember. There is our commission, [*Giving it.*]
    From which we would not have you warp.—Call hither,
    I say, bid come before us, Angelo.—

[*Exit an* ATTENDANT.]

    What figure of us think you he will bear?
    For you must know we have with special soul
    Elected him our absence to supply;
    Lent him our terror, dress'd him with our love,
    And given his deputation all the organs

---

[1] "Am put to *know*" is the same, I take it, as am *given* or *made* to *understand.* We have a like expression in *Cymbeline,* ii. 3: "I am much sorry, sir, you *put me* to forget a lady's manners."

[2] *Lists* is *limits* or *boundaries.* So in *Hamlet,* iv. 2: "The ocean, over-peering of his *list,* eats not the flats with more impetuous haste," &c.

[3] All that Escalus needs, to complete his fitness for the duties in question, is *legal* sufficiency, that is, *authority.* So that the meaning of the whole clause seems to be, "Then no more remains but to add *authority commensurate* with your worth," or, "*as ample* as is your worth." This use of *sufficiency* in the sense of *authority* or *full power* is rare; but we have a like instance in Bacon's Essay *Of Seeming Wise*: "For, as the apostle saith of godliness,' Having a show of godliness, but denying the power thereof; so certainly there are, in points of wisdom and *sufficiency,* that do nothing or a little very solemnly; *magna conatu nugas.*"

[4] *Pregnant,* here, is *ripe,* well-informed, or *full of learning* and experience.—"The terms for common justice" are, probably, the forms and technical language of the law.

Of our own power: what think you of it?
ESCALUS. If any in Vienna be of worth
    To undergo such ample grace and Honour,
    It is Lord Angelo.
DUKE. Look where he comes.

[*Enter* ANGELO.]

ANGELO. Always obedient to your grace's will,
    I come to know your pleasure.
DUKE. Angelo,
    There is a kind of character in thy life
    That to th' observer doth thy history
    Fully unfold.[5] Thyself and thy belongings
    Are not thine own so proper,[6] as to waste
    Thyself upon thy virtues, they on thee.
    Heaven doth with us as we with torches do,
    Not light them for themselves: for if our virtues
    Did not go forth of us, 'twere all alike
    As if we had them not. Spirits are not finely touch'd
    But to fine issues;[7] nor nature never lends
    The smallest scruple of her excellence
    But, like a thrifty goddess, she determines
    Herself the glory of a creditor,
    Both thanks and use.[8] But I do bend my speech

---

[5] The Duke here speaks as knowing Angelo's real character, and at the same time as believing him to be what he seems. This makes his speech somewhat enigmatical, and gives it an air of meaning more than meets the ear. So the leading idea appears to be, that Angelo has something about him that signs him for eminence; that to a well-seeing eye the born statesman and ruler are legible in his bearing; that his life indicates certain latent aptitudes fitting him and pointing him out for high trust and prerogative: so that, if he be but transferred to his proper sphere, the germs of greatness in him will soon come to blossom. Thus, to one who reads him aright, there is a peculiarity in his life, a moral idiom, that prognosticates for him a history full of renown. All this, to be sure, is ironical; but, in itself, and in the way it is put, it is perfectly suited to the Duke's purpose of drawing Angelo out, and so unmasking him.

[6] That is, so *peculiarly* or *exclusively* thine own *property.*

[7] "Touch'd to fine issues" is kindled or quickened to noble ends, to lofty purposes, or by great occasions. A just and felicitous thought, well illustrated in Wordsworth's *Character of the Happy Warrior*:

    But who, if he be call'd upon to face
    Some awful moment to which Heaven has join'd
    Great issues, good or bad for human kind,
    Is happy as a lover; and attired
    With sudden brightness, like a man inspired.

[8] *Use* is *interest*, returns of *profit* or *advantage.*

To one that can my part in him advertise;[9]
Hold, therefore, Angelo; [*Tendering his commission.*]
In our remove be thou at full ourself:
Mortality and mercy in Vienna
Live in thy tongue and heart! Old Escalus,
Though first in question, is thy secondary:
Take thy commission. [*Giving it.*]

ANGELO. Now, good my lord,
Let there be some more test made of my metal,
Before so noble and so great a figure
Be stamp'd upon it.

DUKE. No more evasion:
We have with a leaven'd[10] and prepared choice
Proceeded to you; therefore take your honours.
Our haste from hence is of so quick condition
That it prefers itself, and leaves unquestion'd
Matters of needful value. We shall write to you
As time and our concernings shall importune,
How it goes with us; and do look to know
What doth befall you here. So, fare you well:
To the hopeful execution do I leave you
Of your commissions.

ANGELO. Yet give leave, my lord,
That we may bring you[11] something on the way.

DUKE. My haste may not admit it;
Nor need you, on mine Honour, have to do
With any scruple: your scope is as mine own:
So to enforce or qualify the laws
As to your soul seems good. Give me your hand;
I'll privily away: I love the people,
But do not like to stage me to their eyes:
Though it do well, I do not relish well
Their loud applause and aves[12] vehement:
Nor do I think the man of safe discretion

---

[9] "To one who is himself competent to instruct or counsel others in the very part, that is, the matter, in which I am instructing him." The Poet often uses to *bend* for to direct. He also has *advertise* repeatedly as here explained. See the last scene of this play, note 270.

[10] *Leaven'd* is *mature*, or *well-considered.* Probably an implied image or idea of ale *well fermented*, and so made fit for use.

[11] "*Bring* you" is *attend* or *escort* you. So *bring* is often used.

[12] *Aves* are *hailings.*—Here the Duke appears to be covertly searching Angelo's sly arts of popularity. Ostensibly he acts a strange part in the play; but these dim intimations of his secret purpose, when duly heeded, make his course appear more rational and judicious. His action is not a whim or caprice, but a shrewd fitting of means to a foreconceived end.

That does affect it. Once more, fare you well.

ANGELO. The Heavens give safety to your purposes!

ESCALUS. Lead forth and bring you back in happiness.

DUKE. I thank you. Fare you well. [*Exit.*]

ESCALUS. I shall desire you, sir, to give me leave
    To have free speech with you; and it concerns me
    To look into the bottom of my place:[13]
    A pow'r I have, but of what strength and nature
    I am not yet instructed.

ANGELO. 'Tis so with me.—Let us withdraw together,
    And we may soon our satisfaction have
    Touching that point.

ESCALUS. I'll wait upon your Honour. [*Exeunt.*]

SCENE II.

A Street.

[*Enter* LUCIO *and two* GENTLEMEN.]

LUCIO. If the Duke, with the other dukes, come not to composition with the King of Hungary, why then all the dukes fall upon the king.

FIRST GENTLEMAN. Heaven grant us its peace, but not the King of Hungary's!

SECOND GENTLEMAN. Amen.

LUCIO. Thou concludest like the sanctimonious pirate that went to sea with the ten commandments, but scraped one out of the table.

SECOND GENTLEMAN.
    Thou shalt not steal?

LUCIO. Ay, that he razed.

FIRST GENTLEMAN. Why, 'twas a commandment to command the captain and all the rest from their functions; they put forth to steal. There's not a soldier of us all that, in the thanksgiving before meat, do relish the petition well that prays for peace.

SECOND GENTLEMAN. I never heard any soldier dislike it.

LUCIO. I believe thee; for I think thou never wast where grace was said.

SECOND GENTLEMAN. No? A dozen times at least.

FIRST GENTLEMAN. What? in metre?

LUCIO. In any proportion[14] or in any language.

---

[13] That is, "ascertain fully where I am, and what is the nature and scope of my office." To look to the bottom of a thing, is to *see through* it.

[14] *Proportion*, here, is *measure* or *metre*.

FIRST GENTLEMAN. I think, or in any religion.

LUCIO. Ay! why not? Grace is grace, despite of all controversy. As, for example;—thou thyself art a wicked villain, despite of all grace.

FIRST GENTLEMAN. Well, there went but a pair of shears between us.[15]

LUCIO. I grant; as there may between the lists and the velvet. Thou art the list.

FIRST GENTLEMAN. And thou the velvet: thou art good velvet; thou'rt a three-piled piece, I warrant thee: I had as lief be a list of an English kersey as be piled, as thou art piled, for a French velvet.[16] Do I speak feelingly now?

LUCIO. I think thou dost; and, indeed, with most painful feeling of thy speech. I will, out of thine own confession, learn to begin thy health; but, whilst I live, forget to drink after thee.[17]

FIRST GENTLEMAN. I think I have done myself wrong; have I not?

SECOND GENTLEMAN. Yes, that thou hast, whether thou art tainted or free.[18]

[*Enter* MISTRESS OVERDONE.]

LUCIO. Behold, behold, where Madam Mitigation comes! I have purchased as many diseases under her roof as come to—

SECOND GENTLEMAN. To what, I pray?

FIRST GENTLEMAN. Judge.

SECOND GENTLEMAN. To three thousand dolours[19] a year.

FIRST GENTLEMAN. Ay, and more.

LUCIO. A French crown more.

FIRST GENTLEMAN. Thou art always figuring diseases in me, but thou art full of error; I am sound.

LUCIO. Nay, not, as one would say, healthy; but so sound as things that are hollow: thy bones are hollow: impiety has made a feast of thee.

---

[15] A proverbial phrase; meaning "we were cut out of the same piece." The proverb is still current.

[16] A quibble between *piled* and *pilled* or *peeled.* Velvet was prized according to *the pile, three-piled* being the richest.—*But piled* or *pilled* also meant *bald.* The jest alludes to the loss of hair in what was called the French disease.—English *kersey* was a cheap coarse woollen cloth, worn by plain people.

[17] Lucio, finding that the Gentleman understands him so well, promises to drink his health, but to avoid *drinking after* him, as the cup of an infected person was thought to be contagious.

[18] The Poet often uses *free* in the sense of *pure, undefiled,* or *innocent.* Here it means *untainted* with the disease in question.

[19] A quibble between *dolours* and *dollars,* the former meaning *pains.* The Poet has the equivoque several times.

[*Enter* MISTRESS OVERDONE.]

FIRST GENTLEMAN. How now! which of your hips has the most profound sciatica?

MISTRESS OVERDONE. Well, well; there's one yonder arrested and carried to prison was worth five thousand of you all.

FIRST GENTLEMAN. Who's that, I pray thee?

MISTRESS OVERDONE. Marry, sir, that's Claudio, Signior Claudio.

FIRST GENTLEMAN. Claudio to prison! 'tis not so.

MISTRESS OVERDONE. Nay, but I know 'tis so: I saw him arrested; saw him carried away; and, which is more, within these three days his head to be chopped off.

LUCIO. But, after all this fooling, I would not have it so. Art thou sure of this?

MISTRESS OVERDONE. I am too sure of it: and it is for getting Madam Julietta with child.

LUCIO. Believe me, this may be: he promised to meet me two hours since, and he was ever precise in promise-keeping.

SECOND GENTLEMAN. Besides, you know, it draws something near to the speech we had to such a purpose.

FIRST GENTLEMAN. But most of all agreeing with the proclamation.

LUCIO. Away; let's go learn the truth of it.

[*Exeunt* LUCIO *and* GENTLEMEN.]

MISTRESS OVERDONE. Thus, what with the war, what with the sweat,[20] what with the gallows, and what with poverty, I am custom-shrunk.—

[*Enter* POMPEY.]

How now! what's the news with you?

POMPEY. Yonder man is carried to prison.

MISTRESS OVERDONE. Well: what has he done?

POMPEY. A woman.

MISTRESS OVERDONE. But what's his offence?

POMPEY. Groping for trouts in a peculiar river.

MISTRESS OVERDONE. What! is there a maid with child by him?

POMPEY. No; but there's a woman with maid by him. You have not heard of the proclamation, have you?

---

[20] Some think this refers to the curative process, what was called the *sweating-tub*, then used for the disease mentioned before. Dyce, however, in his *Glossary*, says, "Here, it would seem, the *sweat* means the sweating sickness, and not the method used for the cure of the venereal disease."

MISTRESS OVERDONE. What proclamation, man?

POMPEY. All houses in the suburbs[21] of Vienna must be plucked down.

MISTRESS OVERDONE. And what shall become of those in the city?

POMPEY. They shall stand for seed: they had gone down too, but that a wise burgher put in for them.

MISTRESS OVERDONE. But shall all our houses of resort in the suburbs be pulled down?

POMPEY. To the ground, mistress.

MISTRESS OVERDONE. Why, here's a change indeed in the commonwealth! What shall[22] become of me?

POMPEY. Come, fear not you; good counsellors lack no clients: though you change your place you need not change your trade; I'll be your tapster still. Courage; there will be pity taken on you: you that have worn your eyes almost out in the service, you will be considered.

MISTRESS OVERDONE. What's to do here, Thomas Tapster?[23] Let's withdraw.

POMPEY. Here comes Signior Claudio, led by the Provost to prison: and there's Madam Juliet. [*Exeunt.*]

[*Enter* the PROVOST, CLAUDIO, JULIET, *and* OFFICERS.]

CLAUDIO. [*To the* PROVOST.] Fellow, why dost thou show me thus to the world?
Bear me to prison, where I am committed.

PROVOST. I do it not in evil disposition,
But from Lord Angelo by special charge.

CLAUDIO. Thus can the demi-god Authority
Make us pay down for our offence[24] by weight.
The words of Heaven;—on whom it will, it will;
On whom it will not, so; yet still 'tis just.

[*Re-enter* LUCIO *and the two* GENTLEMEN.]

LUCIO. Why, how now, Claudio, whence comes this restraint?

CLAUDIO. From too much liberty, my Lucio, liberty:
As surfeit is the father of much fast,

---

[21] In one of the Scotch laws of James it is ordered, "that *common women* be put at the utmost endes of townes, queire least peril of fire is."

[22] *Shall* where present usage would require *will*. The two were often used interchangeably.

[23] *Thomas*, it appears, was a common name for a *tapster* by trade.

[24] Offence' for *offences*. The Poet often has words thus elided, with an (') to mark the plural sense.

So every scope by the immoderate use
Turns to restraint. Our natures do pursue,
Like rats that raven down their proper bane,
A thirsty evil; and when we drink we die.[25]

LUCIO. If I could speak so wisely under an arrest, I would send for
certain of my creditors; and yet, to say the truth, I had as lief have
the foppery of freedom as the morality of imprisonment.—What's
thy offence, Claudio?

CLAUDIO. What but to speak of would offend again.

LUCIO. What, is't murder?

CLAUDIO. No.

LUCIO. Lechery?

CLAUDIO. Call it so.

PROVOST. Away, sir; you must go.

CLAUDIO. One word, good friend.—Lucio, a word with you.

[Takes him aside.]

LUCIO. A hundred, if they'll do you any good. Is lechery so looked
after?

CLAUDIO. Thus stands it with me:—Upon a true contráct[26]
I got possessïön[27] of Julietta's bed:
You know the lady; she is fast my wife,
Save that we do th'[28] denunciation[29] lack
Of outward order: this we came not to

---

[25] To *ravin down* is to *devour ravenously.* The Poet has *ravin up* in the same sense,
in *Macbeth,* ii. 2.—The text is well illustrated from Chapman's *Revenge for Honour:*

> Like poison'd rats, which, when they've swallow'd
> The pleasing bane, rest not until they *drink,*
> And can rest then much less, until they burst.

[26] This "true contract" was a formal betrothment or troth-plight, formerly much
practised, and recognized in law, as having the force of a marriage, though not as
conferring the nuptials. The Poet sets forth an apt instance of it between Olivia and
Sebastian in *Twelfth Night.*

[27] The endings -*ion* and -ian, and also -*ious* and -*ience,* not to mention others, were
often used as dissyllabic. Here *possession* is meant to be four syllables. The Poet abounds
in similar instances; though they more commonly occur at the ends of his lines; as a little
after in this scene: "And there receive her *approbation?*

[28] The Poet often thus elides *the* so as to make it coalesce with the preceding word
into one syllable. So "*to th'* world" a little before in this scene. And we have many other
like instances, as *all th', at th', in th', by th', for th', from th';* also, sometimes a double
elision, as *with'* for *with the.* The usage is much more frequent in his later plays, though it
occurs occasionally in the earlier. Nearly all the modern editors ignore it.

[29] *Denounce* and its derivatives were sometimes used in the sense of *publish* or
announce. So in Hall's *Cases of Conscience:* "This publick and reiterated *denunciation* of
banns before matrimony.' And Shakespeare must have often found the phrase
"*denouncing* war" in his favourite historian, Holinshed.

Only for propagation[30] of a dower
Remaining in the coffer of her friends;
From whom we thought it meet to hide our love
Till time had made them for us. But it chances
The stealth of our most mutual entertainment,
With character too gross, is writ on Juliet.
LUCIO. With child, perhaps?
CLAUDIO. Unhappily, even so.
And the new deputy now for the Duke,—
Whether it be the fault and glimpse of newness,
Or whether that the body public be
A horse whereon the governor doth ride,
Who, newly in the seat, that it may know
He can command, lets it straight feel the spur:
Whether the tyranny be in his place,
Or in his eminence that fills it up,
I stagger in:—but this new governor
Awakes me all the enrolled penalties
Which have, like unscour'd armour, hung by the wall
So long that nineteen zodiacs[31] have gone round
And none of them been worn; and, for a name,
Now puts the drowsy and neglected act
Freshly on me; 'tis surely for a name.
LUCIO. I warrant it is: and thy head stands so tickle[32] on thy shoulders
that a milkmaid, if she be in love, may sigh it off. Send after the
Duke, and appeal to him.
CLAUDIO. I have done so, but he's not to be found.
I pr'ythee, Lucio, do me this kind service:
This day my sister should the cloister enter,
And there receive her approbation:[33]
Acquaint her with the danger of my state;
Implore her, in my voice, that she make friends
To the strict deputy; bid herself assay him;
I have great hope in that: for in her youth
There is a prone[34] and speechless dialect

---

[30] Rather an odd use of *propagation*, but probably meaning *continuance*, or *increase*. The Poet has to *propagate* at least twice in the sense of to *increase*. So in *Romeo and Juliet*, i. 1: "Griefs of mine own lie heavy in my breast, which thou wilt *propagate*, to have it prest with more of thine." And in *Timon of Athens*, i. 1: "All kind of natures, that labour on the bosom of this sphere *to propagate* their states."

[31] *Zodiacs* for *years*, or *Has yearly courses* of the Sun.

[32] *Tickle* here means *unsteady* or *tottering*. So in *2 Henry VI.*, i. 1: "Anjou and Maine are given to the French; Paris is lost; the state of Normandy stands on a *tickle* point, now they are gone."

[33] "*Receive* her *approbation*" is enter upon her *probationary term*, that is, her noviciate.

Such as moves men; beside, she hath prosperous art
When she will play with reason and discourse,
And well she can persuade.

LUCIO. I pray she may; as well for the encouragement of the like,
which else would stand under grievous imposition, as for the
enjoying of thy life, who I would be sorry should be thus foolishly
lost at a game of tick-tack.[35] I'll to her.

CLAUDIO. I thank you, good friend Lucio.

LUCIO. Within two hours—

CLAUDIO. Come, officer, away. [*Exeunt.*]

SCENE III.

A Monastery.

[*Enter* DUKE *and Friar* THOMAS.]

DUKE. No; holy father; throw away that thought;
Believe not that the dribbling[36] dart of love
Can pierce a complete bosom: why I desire thee
To give me secret harbour hath a purpose
More grave and wrinkled than the aims and ends
Of burning youth.

FRIAR. May your grace speak of it?

DUKE. My holy sir, none better knows than you
How I have ever lov'd the life remov'd,
And held in idle price to haunt assemblies
Where youth, and cost, a witless bravery keep.[37]
I have deliver'd to Lord Angelo—
A man of stricture[38] and firm abstinence—
My absolute power and place here in Vienna,
And he supposes me travell'd to Poland;
For so I have strew'd it in the common ear,
And so it is received. Now, pious sir,

---

[34] *Prone* is *apt, ready, prompt*; though Mr. White takes it here in the sense of *humble.* The meaning of the passage seems to be, "There is an apt and silent eloquence in her looks, such as moves men."

[35] *Tick-tack* was a game played with tables, something like *backgammon.* So the French has an old phrase, "Jouer au *tric-trac*," also used in a wanton sense.

[36] According to Richardson, *dribble* is a diminutive of *drib*, from *drip*, and means doing a thing "by drips or drops." *Dribber* appears also to have been a term of contempt in archery. So Roger Ascham, in his *Toxophilus*: "If he give it over, and not use to shoote truly, he shall become, of a fayre archer, a starke squirter and *dribber.*"

[37] *Bravery*, here, is *finery in apparel, gay, showy dress.* Repeatedly so.—*Keep* is *dwell, lodge,* or *haunt*; also a frequent usage.

[38] *Stricture* for *strictness*, evidently. Not so elsewhere, I think.

> You will demand of me why I do this?
> FRIAR. Gladly, my lord.
> DUKE. We have strict statutes and most biting laws,—
>   The needful bits and curbs to headstrong steeds,—
>   Which for this fourteen years[39] we have let sleep,
>   Even like an o'ergrown lion in a cave,
>   That goes not out to prey. Now, as fond fathers,
>   Having bound up the threat'ning twigs of birch,
>   Only to stick it in their children's sight
>   For terror, not to use, in time the rod
>   Becomes more mock'd than fear'd; so our decrees,
>   Dead to infliction, to themselves are dead;
>   And liberty plucks justice by the nose;
>   The baby beats the nurse, and quite athwart
>   Goes all decorum.
> FRIAR. It rested in your grace
>   To unloose this tied-up justice when you pleas'd;
>   And it in you more dreadful would have seem'd
>   Than in Lord Angelo.
> DUKE. I do fear, too dreadful:
>   Sith 'twas my fault to give the people scope,
>   'Twould be my tyranny to strike and gall them
>   For what I bid them do: for we bid this be done
>   When evil deeds have their permissive pass
>   And not the punishment. Therefore, indeed, my father,
>   I have on Angelo impos'd the office;
>   Who may, in the ambush of my name, strike home,
>   And yet my nature never in the fight
>   To do in slander.[40] And to behold his sway,
>   I will, as 'twere a brother of your order,
>   Visit both prince and people: therefore, I pr'ythee,
>   Supply me with the habit, and instruct me
>   How I may formally in person bear me
>   Like a true friar. Moe reasons for this action
>   At our more leisure shall I render you;
>   Only, this one:—Lord Angelo is precise;
>   Stands at a guard with envy;[41] scarce confesses

---

[39] In the preceding scene, "nineteen zodiacs" is mentioned as the period during which the "biting laws" have been suffered to sleep. Was this an oversight of the Poet's? Dyce thinks "there can be little doubt" that either *fourteen* should be *nineteen* here, or that *nineteen* in the former passage should be *fourteen*.

[40] The Duke's purpose, as here set forth, apparently is, to avoid any open contest with crime, where his efforts would expose him to slander; or not to let his *person* be seen in the fight, where he would have to *do*, that is, to *act*, in the face of detraction and censure.

That his blood flows, or that his appetite
Is more to bread than stone: hence shall we see,
If power change purpose, what our seemers be. [*Exeunt.*]

SCENE IV.

A Nunnery.

[*Enter* ISABELLA *and* FRANCISCA.]

ISABELLA. And have you nuns no further privileges?
FRANCISCA. Are not these large enough?
ISABELLA. Yes, truly; I speak not as desiring more,
    But rather wishing a more strict restraint
    Upon the sisterhood, the votarists of Saint Clare.
LUCIO. [*Within.*] Ho! Peace be in this place!
ISABELLA. Who's that which calls?
FRANCISCA. It is a man's voice. Gentle Isabella,
    Turn you the key, and know his business of him;
    You may, I may not; you are yet unsworn:
    When you have vow'd, you must not speak with men
    But in the presence of the prioress;
    Then, if you speak, you must not show your face;
    Or, if you show your face, you must not speak.
    He calls again; I pray you answer him. [*Exit.*]
ISABELLA. Peace and prosperity! Who is't that calls?

[*Enter* LUCIO.]

LUCIO. Hail, virgin, if you be,—as those cheek-roses
    Proclaim you are no less! Can you so stead me
    As bring me to the sight of Isabella,
    A novice of this place, and the fair sister
    To her unhappy brother Claudio?
ISABELLA. *Why her unhappy brother*? let me ask;
    The rather, for I now must make you know
    I am that Isabella, and his sister.
LUCIO. Gentle and fair, your brother kindly greets you:
    Not to be weary with you, he's in prison.
ISABELLA. Woe me! For what?
LUCIO. For that which, if myself might be his judge,

---

[41] That is, stands on his guard *against malice* or *malicious tongues. Malice* is the more common meaning of *envy* in old English. It is clear, from this passage, that the Duke distrusts Angelo's professions of sanctity, and is laying plans to unmask him.

He should receive his punishment in thanks:
He hath got his friend with child.
ISABELLA. Sir, make me not your story.
LUCIO. 'Tis true.
    I would not—though 'tis my familiar sin
    With maids to seem the lapwing,[42] and to jest,
    Tongue far from heart—play with all virgins so:
    I hold you as a thing ensky'd and sainted;
    By your renouncement an immortal spirit;
    And to be talk'd with in sincerity,
    As with a saint.
ISABELLA. You do blaspheme the good in mocking me.
LUCIO. Do not believe it. Fewness and truth,[43] 'tis thus:
    Your brother and his lover have embraced:
    As those that feed grow full: as blossoming time,
    That from the seedness the bare fallow brings
    To teeming foison;[44] even so her plenteous womb
    Expresseth his full tilth and husbandry.
ISABELLA. Some one with child by him?—My cousin Juliet?
LUCIO. Is she your cousin?
ISABELLA. Adoptedly, as school-maids change[45] their names
    By vain though apt affection.
LUCIO. She it is.
ISABELLA. O, let him marry her!
LUCIO. This is the point.
    The Duke is very strangely gone from hence;
    Bore many gentlemen, myself being one,
    In hand,[46] and hope of action: but we do learn
    By those that know the very nerves of state,
    His givings out were of an infinite distance
    From his true-meant design. Upon his place,
    And with full line of his authority,
    Governs Lord Angelo: a man whose blood
    Is very snow-broth; one who never feels
    The wanton stings and motions of the sense.
    But doth rebate[47] and blunt his natural edge

---

[42] The lapwing cries most, farthest from her nest," is an old proverb.

[43] That is, *in few and true words*; or, *briefly* and *truly*.

[44] *Foison* is *plenty, abundance,* or *rich harvest.* Repeatedly so.—*Seedness,* if the text be right, must mean *seed-time, seeding,* or *sowing.* The word does not occur again in Shakespeare.

[45] *Change* for *exchange* or *interchange.* So in *Hamlet*, i. 2: "Sir, my good friend; I'll *change* that name with you."

[46] To *bear in hand* was a phrase in frequent use, meaning to *keep in expectation,* to *amuse and lead along with false hopes.* The Poet has it often. So in *2 Henry IV.*, i. 2: "A rascally yea-forsooth knave, to *bear a gentleman in hand,* and then stand upon security!"

With profits of the mind, study, and fast.
He,—to give fear to use and liberty,[48]
Which have for long run by the hideous law,
As mice by lions,—hath pick'd out an act,
Under whose heavy sense your brother's life
Falls into forfeit: he arrests him on it;
And follows close the rigour of the statute
To make him an example; all hope is gone.
Unless you have the grace by your fair prayer
To soften Angelo: and that's my pith
Of business 'twixt you and your poor brother.
ISABELLA. Doth he so seek his life?
LUCIO. 'Has censured[49] him
    Already; and, as I hear, the Provost hath
    A warrant for his execution.
ISABELLA. Alas! what poor ability's in me
    To do him good.
LUCIO. Assay the power you have.
ISABELLA. My power! alas, I doubt,—
LUCIO. Our doubts are traitors,
    And make us lose the good we oft might win
    By fearing to attempt. Go to Lord Angelo,
    And let him learn to know, when maidens sue,
    Men give like gods; but when they weep and kneel,
    All their petitions are as freely theirs
    As they themselves would owe[50] them.
ISABELLA. I'll see what I can do.
LUCIO. But speedily.
ISABELLA. I will about it straight;
    No longer staying but to give the Mother
    Notice of my affair. I humbly thank you:
    Commend me to my brother: soon at night[51]
    I'll send him certain word of my success.[52]
LUCIO. I take my leave of you.
ISABELLA. Good sir, adieu. [*Exeunt.*]

---

[47] To *rebate* is to *beat back*, and so *make dull.*
[48] To put the restraint of fear upon licentious habit and abused freedom.
[49] To *censure* is to judge, or to *pass sentence.* So again in the next scene.
[50] *Owe* is *possess* or *own.* So the Poet continually.
[51] *Soon at night* is *about* or *towards* night.
[52] *Success* in the Latin sense; the *sequel, issue,* or *result* of any thing.

ACT II.

SCENE I.

A Hall in ANGELO's *House.*

[*Enter* ANGELO, ESCALUS, *and a* JUSTICE, *the* PROVOST,[53] OFFICERS, *and others attending.*]

ANGELO. We must not make a scarecrow of the law,
  Setting it up to fear[54] the birds of prey,
  And let it keep one shape till custom make it
  Their perch, and not their terror.
ESCALUS. Ay, but yet
  Let us be keen, and rather cut a little
  Than fall,[55] and bruise to death. Alas! this gentleman,
  Whom I would save, had a most noble father.
  Let but your Honour know,—
  Whom I believe to be most strait in virtue,—
  That, in the working of your own affections,
  Had time coher'd with place, or place with wishing,
  Or that the resolute acting of your blood
  Could have attain'd th' effect of your own purpose,
  Whether you had not sometime in your life
  Err'd in this point which now you censure him,
  And pull'd the law upon you.
ANGELO. 'Tis one thing to be tempted, Escalus,
  Another thing to fall. I not deny
  The jury, passing on the prisoner's life,
  May, in the sworn twelve, have a thief or two
  Guiltier than him they try. What's open made to justice,
  That justice seizes. What knows the laws
  That thieves do pass[56] on thieves? 'Tis very pregnant,[57]
  The jewel that we find, we stoop and take it,
  Because we see it; but what we do not see
  We tread upon, and never think of it.
  You may not so extenuate his offence
  For[58] I have had such faults; but rather tell me,

---

[53] *Provost* was used for the *principal* or *president* of any establishment. Here a *jailor.*
[54] To *fear* was often used as an active verb; to *frighten* or *terrify.*
[55] *Fall* is here used as a causative verb; to *throw down*, to *make* or *let fall.* Often so.
[56] An old forensic term, meaning to *pass judgment* or *sentence.*
[57] *Pregnant*, here, is *full of proof*, or *self-evident.* Repeatedly so.

When I, that censure him, do so offend,
Let mine own judgment pattern out my death,
And nothing come in partial. Sir, he must die.
ESCALUS. Be't as your wisdom will.
ANGELO. Where is the Provost?
PROVOST. [*Coming forward.*] Here, if it like your Honour.[59]
ANGELO. See that Claudio
Be executed by nine to-morrow morning:
Bring him his confessor; let him be prepard;
For that's the utmost of his pilgrimage.

[*Exit* PROVOST.]

ESCALUS. Well, Heaven forgive him! and forgive us all!
Some rise by sin, and some by virtue fall:
Some run from brakes of vice, and answer none,
And some condemned for a fault alone.[60]

[*Enter* ELBOW, *and* OFFICERS *with* FROTH *and* POMPEY.]

ELBOW. Come, bring them away: if these be good people in a commonweal that do nothing but use their abuses in common houses, I know no law; bring them away.
ANGELO. How now, sir! What's your name? and what's the matter?
ELBOW. If it please your Honour, I am the poor Duke's constable,[61] and my name is Elbow; I do lean upon justice, sir, and do bring in

---

[58] This use of *for* with the sense of *because* was very common in all sorts of writing.

[59] "If *it please* your Honour," or, "If your Honour *like* it." The phrase was much used in the Poet's time.

[60] The general sense of this strange passage evidently is, that some, who are hardened in sin by a long course of evil-doing, escape scot-free, and are never called to account, while others, for a fault *only*, or for a *single* fault, are visited with extreme punishment. But the particular meaning of the word *brakes* is, to say the least, very doubtful. It is commonly explained *brambles*, *thickets*, or *thorny entanglements*. So the word appears to be used in *Henry VIII.*, i. 2: "'Tis the fate of place, and the rough *brake* that virtue must go through." Also in Beaumont and Fletcher's *Thierry and Theodoret*, v. 1: "These be honourable adventures! had I that honest blood in my veins again, Queen, that your feats and these frights have drain'd from me, honour should pull hard, ere it drew me into these *brakes*." On the other hand, the word was sometimes used for an *engine of torture*; also for a *trap* or *snare*; which latter seems to be the meaning in Cavendish's *Life of Wolsey*: "Divers of the great estates and Lords of the Council lay in await with my Lady Anne Boleyn, to espy a convenient time and occasion to take the Cardinal in a *brake*." The word was also used in several other senses; and Richardson defines it generally as signifying "any thing which restrains, holds, or keeps in, confines, curbs, tames, subdues." I am not quite clear which of these senses, or indeed whether any of them be the right one in the text.

[61] Meant as a characteristic blunder of Elbow's for "the Duke's poor constable." Dogberry makes the same blunder in *Much Ado*, iii. 5: "We are the poor Duke's officers."

here before your good Honour two notorious benefactors.

ANGELO. Benefactors! Well; what benefactors are they? are they not malefactors?

ELBOW. If it please your Honour, I know not well what they are; but precise villains they are, that I am sure of; and void of all profanation in the world that good Christians ought to have.

ESCALUS. This comes off well;[62] here's a wise officer.

ANGELO. Go to;—what quality are they of? Elbow is your name? Why dost thou not speak, Elbow?

POMPEY. He cannot, sir; he's out at elbow.

ANGELO. What are you, sir?

ELBOW. He, sir? a tapster, sir; parcel-bawd;[63] one that serves a bad woman; whose house, sir, was, as they say, plucked down in the suburbs; and now she professes a hot-house,[64] which, I think, is a very ill house too.

ESCALUS. How know you that?

ELBOW. My wife, sir, whom I detest[65] before Heaven and your Honour,—

ESCALUS. How! thy wife!

ELBOW. Ay, sir; who, I thank Heaven, is an honest woman,—

ESCALUS. Dost thou detest her therefore?

ELBOW. I say, sir, I will detest myself also, as well as she, that this house, if it be not a bawd's house, it is pity of her life, for it is a naughty house.

ESCALUS. How dost thou know that, constable?

ELBOW. Marry, sir, by my wife; who, if she had been a woman cardinally given, might have been accused in fornication, adultery, and all uncleanliness there.

ESCALUS. By the woman's means?

ELBOW. Ay, sir, by Mistress Overdone's means: but as she spit in his face, so she defied him.

POMPEY. Sir, if it please your Honour, this is not so.

ELBOW. Prove it before these varlets here, thou honourable man, prove it.

ESCALUS. [*To* ANGELO.] Do you hear how he misplaces?

POMPEY. Sir, she came in great with child; and longing,—saving your Honour's reverence—for stew'd prunes; sir, we had but two in the

---

[62] An old phrase, meaning "this is a fine showing," or "this is well told"; ironical here, of course.

[63] *Parcel bawd* is *partly bawd.* Shakespeare often uses *parcel* thus for *part*; as, "a *parcel-gilt* goblet," and, "the lips is *parcel* of the mouth." Pompey's other part is jester or clown.

[64] Professes, or pretends, *to keep* a hot-house. Hot-houses were bagnios supplied with vapour-baths; but under this name other accommodations were often furnished.

[65] *Detest* is an Elbowism for *protest.*

house, which at that very distant[66] time stood, as it were, in a fruit dish, a dish of some three-pence; your honours have seen such dishes; they are not China dishes, but very good dishes.

ESCALUS. Go to, go to; no matter for the dish, sir.

POMPEY. No, indeed, sir, not of a pin; you are therein in the right; but to the point. As I say, this Mistress Elbow, being, as I say, with child, and being great-bellied, and longing, as I said, for prunes; and having but two in the dish, as I said, Master Froth here, this very man, having eaten the rest, as I said, and, as I say, paying for them very honestly;—for, as you know, Master Froth, I could not give you three-pence again,—

FROTH. No, indeed.

POMPEY. Very well; you being then, if you be remember'd, cracking the stones of the foresaid prunes,—

FROTH. Ay, so I did indeed.

POMPEY. Why, very well: I telling you then, if you be remember'd, that such a one and such a one were past cure of the thing you wot of, unless they kept very good diet, as I told you,—

FROTH. All this is true.

POMPEY. Why, very well then.

ESCALUS. Come, you are a tedious fool: to the purpose. What was done to Elbow's wife that he hath cause to complain of? Come me[67] to what was done to her.

POMPEY. Sir, your Honour cannot come to that yet.

ESCALUS. No, sir, nor I mean it not.

POMPEY. Sir, but you shall come to it, by your Honour's leave. And, I beseech you, look into Master Froth here, sir, a man of fourscore pound a-year; whose father died at Hallowmas:—was't not at Hallowmas, Master Froth?

FROTH. All-hallowed eve.[68]

POMPEY. Why, very well; I hope here be truths: He, sir, sitting, as I say, in a lower chair,[69] sir;—'twas in the Bunch of Grapes,[70] where, indeed, you have a delight to sit, have you not?—

FROTH. I have so; because it is an open room, and good for Winter.[71]

POMPEY. Why, very well then;—I hope here be truths.

---

[66] Pompey, catching Elbow's trick of speech, uses *distant* for *instant.*

[67] Here *me* is doubtless an instance of the redundant use of pronouns so frequent in Shakespeare.

[68] The *eve of*, that is, the *evening before*, All-Saint's day.

[69] "A *lower* chair" was an *easy* chair, kept in houses, for sick people, and sometimes occupied by lazy ones.

[70] Some such names were commonly given to rooms in the Poet's time. So, in *I Henry IV.*, ii. 4, we have *Half-moon* and *Pomegranate.*

[71] In the list of persons appended to this play in the folio of 1623, Master Froth is set down as "a foolish Gentleman." It is probably in that character that he uses *Winter* here.

ANGELO. This will last out a night in Russia,
    When nights are longest there: I'll take my leave,
    And leave you to the hearing of the cause;
    Hoping you'll find good cause to whip them all.
ESCALUS. I think no less. Good morrow to your lordship.—

    [*Exit* ANGELO.]

    Now, sir, come on; what was done to Elbow's wife, once more?
POMPEY. Once, sir? there was nothing done to her once.
ELBOW. I beseech you, sir, ask him what this man did to my wife.
POMPEY. I beseech your Honour, ask me.
ESCALUS. Well, sir: what did this gentleman to her?
POMPEY. I beseech you, sir, look in this gentleman's face.—Good
    Master Froth, look upon his Honour; 'tis for a good purpose.—
    Doth your Honour mark his face?
ESCALUS. Ay, sir, very well.
POMPEY. Nay, I beseech you, mark it well.
ESCALUS. Well, I do so.
POMPEY. Doth your Honour see any harm in his face?
ESCALUS. Why, no.
POMPEY. I'll be supposed[72] upon a book his face is the worst thing
    about him. Good then; if his face be the worst thing about him,
    how could Master Froth do the constable's wife any harm? I would
    know that of your Honour.
ESCALUS. He's in the right.—Constable, what say you to it?
ELBOW. First, an it like you, the house is a respected house; next, this
    is a respected fellow; and his mistress is a respected woman.
POMPEY. By this hand, sir, his wife is a more respected person than
    any of us all.
ELBOW. Varlet, thou liest; thou liest, wicked varlet: the time is yet to
    come that she was ever respected with man, woman, or child.
POMPEY. Sir, she was respected with him before he married with her.

---

[72] "I'll be *supposed*" is Pompey's blunder for "I'll be *deposed*" that is, *sworn*;
according to the old practice of requiring witnesses to make oath upon the Bible. As
Pompey is the clown, or "allowed Fool," of the play, his blunders are, of course,
perpetrated in that character. Douce makes the following just note upon him: "The clown
in this play officiates as the tapster of a brothel; whence it has been concluded that he is
not a domestic Fool, nor ought to appear in the dress of that character. A little
consideration will serve to show that the opinion is erroneous; that *this clown* is
altogether a domestic Fool. In ii. 1, Escalus calls him a *tedious Fool*, and *Iniquity*, a name
for one of the old stage buffoons. He tells him that he will have him *whipt*, a punishment
that was very often inflicted on Fools. In *Timon of Athens*, we have a *strumpet's Fool*,
and a similar character is mentioned in the first speech of *Antony and Cleopatra*. But, if
any one should still entertain a doubt on the subject, he may receive the most complete
satisfaction by an attentive examination of ancient prints, many of which will furnish
instances of the common use of the domestic Fool in brothels."

ESCALUS. Which is the wiser here, Justice or Iniquity?[73]—Is this true?

ELBOW. O thou caitiff! O thou varlet! O thou wicked Hannibal! I respected with her before I was married to her!—If ever I was respected with her, or she with me, let not your worship think me the poor Duke's officer.—Prove this, thou wicked Hannibal, or I'll have mine action of battery on thee.

ESCALUS. If he took you a box o' the ear, you might have your action of slander too.

ELBOW. Marry, I thank your good worship for it. What is't your worship's pleasure I should do with this wicked caitiff?

ESCALUS. Truly, officer, because he hath some offences in him that thou wouldst discover if thou couldst, let him continue in his courses till thou knowest what they are.

ELBOW. Marry, I thank your worship for it.—Thou seest, thou wicked varlet, now, what's come upon thee; thou art to continue now, thou varlet; thou art to continue.

ESCALUS. [*To* FROTH.] Where were you born, friend?

FROTH. Here in Vienna, sir.

ESCALUS. Are you of fourscore pounds a-year?

FROTH. Yes, an't please you, sir.

ESCALUS. So.—[*To* POMPEY.] What trade are you of, sir?

POMPEY. A tapster; a poor widow's tapster.

ESCALUS. Your mistress' name?

POMPEY. Mistress Overdone.

ESCALUS. Hath she had any more than one husband?

POMPEY. Nine, sir; Overdone by the last.

ESCALUS. Nine!—Come hither to me, Master Froth. Master Froth, I would not have you acquainted with tapsters: they will draw you, Master Froth, and you will hang them.[74] Get you gone, and let me hear no more of you.

FROTH. I thank your worship. For mine own part, I never come into

---

[73] *Justice* and *Iniquity* were allegorical personages in the old Moral-plays. Iniquity was more commonly called *Vice*, and was, to the Moral-plays, much the same as the licensed jester or allowed Fool was to the later drama. In fact, the dramatic usage of professional Fools in Shakespeare's time grew directly out of that usage of the earlier stage.

[74] Escalus, notwithstanding the dignity of his temper and his office, is genially touched by the ludicrous absurdity of the scene about him, so that he catches the spirit of verbal play. Here we have an equivoque on *draw*; one sense being, "they shall draw liquor for you"; the other, it may be, that of capital offenders being drawn in a cart to the place of execution, or, more likely, the sense of *drawing in*, that is, *cheating* or *swindling*, as in the next speech, "I am *drawn in.*"—*Hang* is here used as a causative verb; the sense being, you shall *cause* them *to be hanged.* This would be done by accusing them, or bearing witness against them, for having swindled him out of money. The Poet uses a good many verbs in that way.

any room in a taphouse but I am drawn in.[75]

ESCALUS. Well, no more of it, Master Froth: farewell.

[*Exit* FROTH.]

—Come you hither to me, master tapster; what's your name,
   master tapster?

POMPEY. Pompey.

ESCALUS. What else?

POMPEY. Bum, sir.

ESCALUS. Troth, and your bum is the greatest thing about you;[76] so
   that, in the beastliest sense, you are Pompey the great. Pompey,
   you are partly a bawd, Pompey, howsoever you colour it in being a
   tapster. Are you not? come, tell me true; it shall be the better for
   you.

POMPEY. Truly, sir, I am a poor fellow that would live.

ESCALUS. How would you live, Pompey? by being a bawd? What do
   you think of the trade, Pompey? is it a lawful trade?

POMPEY. If the law would allow it, sir.

ESCALUS. But the law will not allow it, Pompey: nor it shall not be
   allowed in Vienna.

POMPEY. Does your worship mean to geld and splay[77] all the youth of
   the city?

ESCALUS. No, Pompey.

POMPEY. Truly, sir, in my poor opinion, they will to't then. If your
   worship will take order for the drabs and the knaves, you need not
   to fear the bawds.

ESCALUS. There is pretty orders beginning, I can tell you. It is but
   heading and hanging.

POMPEY. If you head and hang all that offend that way but for ten
   year together, you'll be glad to give out a commission for more
   heads. If this law hold in Vienna ten year, I'll rent the fairest house
   in it, after three-pence a bay:[78] if you live to see this come to pass,
   say Pompey told you so.

ESCALUS. Thank you, good Pompey; and, in requital of your
   prophecy, hark you,—I advise you, let me not find you before me
   again upon any complaint whatsoever, no, not for dwelling where

---

[75] A quibble between the two senses of being induced to enter and of being *cheated*,
as explained in the preceding note.

[76] The fashion for gentlemen has sometimes been, to have the dress swell out as big
as possible about the hips; and perhaps Pompey was intent on making the fashion
ridiculous by exaggeration, or by aping it to excess in his capacity of Fool.

[77] *Splay* is an old form of *spay*; now obsolete.

[78] *After* is here equivalent to *at the rate of. A bay* is an architectural term of not
uncommon occurrence in old descriptions of houses, in reference to the frontage. So in
Coles's *Latin Dictionary*: "*A bay* of building, *Mensura* viginti *quatuor pedum.*"

you do; if I do, Pompey, I shall beat you to your tent, and prove a shrewd Cæsar to you;[79] in plain dealing, Pompey, I shall have you whipt: so for this time, Pompey, fare you well.

POMPEY. I thank your worship for your good counsel; [*Aside.*] but I shall follow it as the flesh and fortune shall better determine.
Whip me! No, no; let carman whip his jade:
The valiant heart's not whipt out of his trade. [*Exit.*]

ESCALUS. Come hither to me, Master Elbow; come hither, Master Constable. How long have you been in this place of constable?

ELBOW. Seven year and a half, sir.

ESCALUS. I thought, by the readiness in the office, you had continued in it some time. You say seven years together?

ELBOW. And a half, sir.

ESCALUS. Alas, it hath been great pains to you! They do you wrong to put you so oft upon't. Are there not men in your ward sufficient to serve it?

ELBOW. Faith, sir, few of any wit in such matters: as they are chosen, they are glad to choose me for them; I do it for some piece of money, and go through with all.

ESCALUS. Look you, bring me in the names of some six or seven, the most sufficient of your parish.

ELBOW. To your worship's house, sir?

ESCALUS. To my house. Fare you well.

[*Exit* ELBOW.]

—What's o'clock, think you?

JUSTICE. Eleven, sir.

ESCALUS. I pray you home to dinner with me.

JUSTICE. I humbly thank you.

ESCALUS. It grieves me for the death of Claudio;
But there's no remedy.

JUSTICE. Lord Angelo is severe.

ESCALUS. It is but needful:
Mercy is not itself that oft looks so;[80]
Pardon is still the nurse of second woe:
But yet, poor Claudio! There's no remedy.—
Come, sir. [*Exeunt.*]

---

[79] Escalus is laughing *inwardly*. He has humour; not so Angelo.
[80] The meaning is, of course, that a frequent pardoning of the guilty is injustice and even cruelty to the innocent.

Scene II.

Another Room in the Same.

[*Enter* PROVOST *and a* SERVANT.]

SERVANT. He's hearing of a cause; he will come straight.
    I'll tell him of you.
PROVOST. Pray you do.

[*Exit* SERVANT.]

—I'll know
His pleasure; may be he will relent. Alas,
He hath but as offended in a dream!
All sects, all ages, smack of this vice; and he
To die for it!

[*Enter* ANGELO.]

ANGELO. Now, what's the matter, Provost?
PROVOST. Is it your will Claudio shall die to-morrow?
ANGELO. Did not I tell thee yea? hadst thou not order?
    Why dost thou ask again?
PROVOST. Lest I might be too rash:
    Under your good correction, I have seen
    When, after execution, judgment hath
    Repented o'er his doom.
ANGELO. Go to; let that be mine:
    Do you your office, or give up your place,
    And you shall well be spared.
PROVOST. I crave your Honour's pardon:
    What shall be done, sir, with the groaning Juliet?
    She's very near her hour.
ANGELO. Dispose of her
    To some more fitter place; and that with speed.

[*Re-enter the* SERVANT.]

SERVANT. Here is the sister of the man condemned
    Desires access to you.
ANGELO. Hath he a sister?
PROVOST. Ay, my good lord; a very virtuous maid,
    And to be shortly of a sisterhood,

If not already.
ANGELO. Well, let her be admitted.—

[*Exit* SERVANT.]

See you the fornicatress be remov'd;
Let her have needful but not lavish means;
There shall be order for it.

[*Enter* LUCIO *and* ISABELLA.]

PROVOST. Save your Honour! [*Offering to retire.*]
ANGELO. Stay a little while.—
    [*To* ISABELLA.] You are welcome: what's your will?
ISABELLA. I am a woeful suitor to your Honour,
    Please but your Honour hear me.
ANGELO. Well; what's your suit?
ISABELLA. There is a vice that most I do abhor,
    And most desire should meet the blow of justice;
    For which I would not plead, but that I must;
    For which I must not plead, but that I am
    At war 'twixt will and will not.
ANGELO. Well; the matter?
ISABELLA. I have a brother is condemn'd to die;
    I do beseech you, let it be his fault,
    And not my brother.[81]
PROVOST. [*Aside.*] Heaven give thee moving graces.
ANGELO. Condemn the fault and not the actor of it!
    Why, every fault's condemn'd ere it be done;
    Mine were the very cipher of a function,
    To find the faults whose fine stands in record,[82]
    And let go by the actor.
ISABELLA. O just but severe law!
    I had a brother, then.—Heaven keep your Honour!

[*Retiring.*]

LUCIO. [*Aside to* ISABELLA.] Give't not o'er so: to him again,
        entreat him;
    Kneel down before him, hang upon his gown;
    You are too cold: if you should need a pin,

---

[81] "Let my brother's fault die, and not my brother himself."
[82] "To punish the fault whose punishment is prescribed in the law," seems to be the meaning here.—In the preceding line, "*very* cipher" is *mere* cipher. The Poet often has very thus. So in *Hamlet*, iv. 4: "A *very* riband in the cap of youth, yet needful too."

   You could not with more tame a tongue desire it:
   To him, I say.
ISABELLA. Must he needs die?
ANGELO. Maiden, no remedy.
ISABELLA. Yes; I do think that you might pardon him,
   And neither Heaven nor man grieve at the mercy.
ANGELO. I will not do't.
ISABELLA. But can you, if you would?
ANGELO. Look, what I will not, that I cannot do.
ISABELLA. But might you do't, and do the world no wrong,
   If so your heart were touch'd with that remorse[83]
   As mine is to him?
ANGELO. He's sentenc'd; 'tis too late.
LUCIO. [*Aside to* ISABELLA.] You are too cold.
ISABELLA. Too late? Why, no; I, that do speak a word,
   May call it back again. Well, believe this,
   No ceremony that to great ones 'longs,
   Not the king's crown nor the deputed sword,
   The marshal's truncheon nor the judge's robe,
   Become them with one half so good a grace
   As mercy does.
   If he had been as you, and you as he,
   You would have slipp'd like him;
   But he, like you, would not have been so stern.
ANGELO. Pray you, be gone.
ISABELLA. I would to Heaven I had your potency,
   And you were Isabel! should it then be thus?
   No; I would tell what 'twere to be a judge
   And what a prisoner.
LUCIO. [*Aside.*] Ay, touch him; there's the vein.
ANGELO. Your brother is a forfeit of the law,
   And you but waste your words.
ISABELLA. Alas! alas!
   Why, all the souls that were were forfeit once;
   And He that might the vantage best have took
   Found out the remedy. How would you be
   If He, which is the top of judgment, should
   But judge you as you are? O, think on that;
   And mercy then will breathe within your lips,
   Like man new-made.[84]
ANGELO. Be you content, fair maid:

---

[83] Here, as usual, *remorse is pity* or *compassion.*
[84] I take our Poet's meaning to be, "If you allow this consideration its due weight, you will find mercy breathing within your lips, as if a new man were formed within you."—HEATH.

It is the law, not I, condemns your brother:
Were he my kinsman, brother, or my son,
It should be thus with him;—he must die to-morrow.
ISABELLA. To-morrow! O, that's sudden! Spare him, spare him!
He's not prepared for death. Even for our kitchens
We kill the fowl of season:[85] shall we serve Heaven
With less respect than we do minister
To our gross selves? Good, good my lord, bethink you:
Who is it that hath died for this offence?
There's many have committed it.
LUCIO. [*Aside to* ISABELLA.] Ay, well said.
ANGELO. The law hath not been dead, though it hath slept:[86]
Those many had not dared to do that evil
If the first that did th' edict infringe
Had answer'd for his deed: now 'tis awake;
Takes note of what is done; and, like a prophet,
Looks in a glass,[87] that shows what future evils,—
Either now, or by remissness new conceiv'd,
And so in progress to be hatch'd and born,—
Are now to have no successive degrees,
But, where they live, to end.
ISABELLA. Yet show some pity.
ANGELO. I show it most of all when I show justice;
For then I pity those I do not know,
Which a dismiss'd offence would after gall;[88]
And do him right that, answering one foul wrong,
Lives not to act another. Be satisfied;
Your brother dies to-morrow; be content.
ISABELLA. So you must be the first that gives this sentence;
And he that suffers. O, 'tis excellent
To have a giant's strength; but it is tyrannous
To use it like a giant.
LUCIO. [*Aside to* ISABELLA.] That's well said.
ISABELLA. Could great men thunder
As Jove himself does, Jove would ne'er be quiet,

---

[85] In *fitting season*; that is, when they are mature or made ready for the purpose. So in *Hamlet*, iii. 3: "Am I, then, revenged to take him in the purging of his soul, when he is fit and *season'd* for the passage?"

[86] *Dormiunt aliquando leges, moriunter nunquam*, is a maxim of English law. Yet it may operate as an *ex-post-facto* law.

[87] Alluding to the magic glasses or charmed mirrors with which witches and fortune-tellers used to reveal the far-off future. In *Macbeth*, iv. 1, the Weird Sisters make use of such a glass to disclose to the hero the long line of kings that is to spring from Banquo.

[88] So in the *Memorials* of Sir Matthew Hale: "When I find myself swayed to mercy, let me remember that there is a mercy likewise due to the country."

For every pelting,[89] petty officer
Would use his Heaven for thunder,—
Nothing but thunder.—Merciful Heaven!
Thou rather, with thy sharp and sulphurous bolt,
Splits the unwedgeable and gnarled oak
Than the soft myrtle; but man, proud man!
Dress'd in a little brief authority,—
Most ignorant of what he's most assured,
His glassy essence,[90]—like an angry ape,
Plays such fantastic tricks before high Heaven
As makes the angels weep; who, with our spleens,
Would all themselves laugh mortal.[91]

LUCIO. [*Aside to* ISABELLA.] O, to him, to him, wench: he will
     relent;
     He's coming; I perceive't.

PROVOST. [*Aside.*] Pray Heaven she win him!

ISABELLA. We cannot weigh our brother with yourself:[92]
     Great men may jest with saints: 'tis wit in them;
     But, in the less, foul profanation.

LUCIO. [*Aside to* ISABELLA.] Thou'rt i' the right, girl; more o' that.

ISABELLA. That in the captain's but a choleric word
     Which in the soldier is flat blasphemy.

LUCIO. [*Aside to* ISABELLA.] Art advised o' that?[93] more on't.

ANGELO. Why do you put these sayings upon me?

ISABELLA. Because authority, though it err like others,
     Hath yet a kind of medicine in itself
     That skins the vice o' the top.[94] Go to your bosom;
     Knock there; and ask your heart what it doth know
     That's like my brother's fault: if it confess
     A natural guiltiness such as is his,
     Let it not sound a thought upon your tongue

---

[89] The Poet repeatedly uses *pelting* for *paltry.* So in *A Midsummer*, ii. 1: "Have every *pelting* river made so proud."

[90] That is, his *brittle, fragile being.* The meaning seems to be, most ignorant of that which *is most certain*, namely, his natural infirmity.

[91] A very mark-worthy saying; meaning that, if the angels had our disposition to splenetic or satirical mirth, the sight of our human arrogance strutting through its absurd antics would cast them into such an ecstasy of ridicule, that they would laugh themselves clean out of their immortality; this celestial prerogative being incompatible with such ebullitions of spleen.

[92] Meaning, apparently, "I cannot *match* or *compare* my brother with you, cannot cast him into the scales as a *counterpoise* to yourself." To jest with one is to be on equal terms with him.

[93] "Have you well considered that?" *Avised* is merely another form of *advised*, which the Poet often uses in the sense of *informed, assured, circumspect.*

[94] This metaphor occurs again in *Hamlet*, iii. 4: "It will but skin and film the ulcerous place."

Against my brother's life.
ANGELO. [*Aside.*] She speaks, and 'tis
    Such sense that my sense breeds with't.[95]—Fare you well.
ISABELLA. Gentle my lord, turn back.
ANGELO. I will bethink me:—Come again to-morrow.
ISABELLA. Hark how I'll bribe you. Good my lord, turn back.
ANGELO. How! bribe me?
ISABELLA. Ay, with such gifts that Heaven shall share with you.
LUCIO. [*Aside to* ISABELLA.] You had marr'd all else.
ISABELLA. Not with fond shekels of the tested gold,
    Or stones, whose rates are either rich or poor
    As fancy values them: but with true prayers,
    That shall be up at Heaven, and enter there,
    Ere sun-rise,—prayers from preserved souls,
    From fasting maids, whose minds are dedicate
    To nothing temporal.
ANGELO. Well; come to me to-morrow.
LUCIO. [*Aside to* ISABELLA.] Go to; 'tis well; away.
ISABELLA. Heaven keep your Honour safe!
ANGELO. [*Aside.*] Amen: for I
    Am that way going to temptation,
    Where prayers cross.[96]
ISABELLA. At what hour to-morrow
    Shall I attend your lordship?
ANGELO. At any time 'fore noon.
ISABELLA. Save your Honour!

[*Exeunt* LUCIO, ISABELLA, *and* PROVOST.]

ANGELO. From thee,—even from thy virtue![97]—
    What's this, what's this? Is this her fault or mine?
    The tempter or the tempted, who sins most? Ha!
    Not she; nor doth she tempt; but it is I
    That, lying by the violet, in the sun
    Do, as the carrion does, not as the flower,

---

[95] "Such sense as breeds a response in my mind."

[96] The petition, "Lead us not into temptation," is here regarded as crossing or *intercepting* the way Angelo is going. He is seeking temptation by appointing another interview. See, however, Angelo's first speech in the next scene but one. Heath explains the passage thus: "'For I am labouring under a temptation of that peculiar and uncommon kind, that prayers, and every other act of piety and virtue, tend to inflame, instead of allaying it.' For it was the very piety and virtue of Isabella that gave an edge to the lust of Angelo."

[97] Isabella has just used "your *Honour*" as his title: he catches at the proper meaning of the word, and goes to reflecting on the danger his honour is in from the course he is taking.

Corrupt with virtuous season.[98] Can it be
That modesty may more betray our sense
Than woman's lightness? Having waste ground enough,
Shall we desire to raze the sanctuary,
And pitch our evils[99] there? O, fie, fie, fie!
What dost thou? or what art thou, Angelo?
Dost thou desire her foully for those things
That make her good? O, let her brother live;
Thieves for their robbery have authority
When judges steal themselves. What! do I love her,
That I desire to hear her speak again
And feast upon her eyes? What is't I dream on?
O cunning enemy, that, to catch a saint,
With saints dost bait thy hook! Most dangerous
Is that temptation that doth goad us on
To sin in loving virtue: never could the strumpet,
With all her double vigour, art, and nature,
Once stir my temper; but this virtuous maid
Subdues me quite.—Ever till now,
When men were fond, I smil'd and wonder'd how. [*Exit.*]

SCENE III.

A Room in a Prison.

[*Enter, severally, the* DUKE, *disguised as a Friar, and the* PROVOST.]

DUKE. Hail to you, Provost!—so I think you are.
PROVOST. I am the Provost. What's your will, good friar?
DUKE. Bound by my charity and my bless'd order,
    I come to visit the afflicted spirits
    Here in the prison: do me the common right
    To let[100] me see them, and to make me know
    The nature of their crimes, that I may minister
    To them accordingly.

---

[98] "Virtuous season" here means the season that matures and unfolds, or brings forth, the virtue in question, the *sweetness* of the flower.

[99] *Evils* is here used in the sense of *offal* or offals. Dyce quotes upon the passage, "It would not be difficult to show that by *evil* or *evils* our forefathers designated *physical* as well as moral corruption and impurity."—The desecration of religious structures by converting them to the lowest uses of nature was an eastern mode of showing contempt. Angelo could hardly have chosen a stronger figure for expressing the heinousness of his intended profligacy.

[100] *To let* is the gerundial infinitive, as it is called, and so is equivalent to *by letting.* A very frequent usage.

PROVOST. I would do more than that, if more were needful.
> Look, here comes one,—a gentlewoman of mine,
> Who, falling in[101] the flaws of her own youth,
> Hath blister'd her report. She is with child;
> And he that got it, sentenced,—a young man
> More fit to do another such offence
> Than die for this.

> [*Enter* JULIET.]

DUKE. When must he die?
PROVOST. As I do think, to-morrow.—
> [*To* JULIET.] I have provided for you; stay awhile
> And you shall be conducted.
DUKE. Repent you, fair one, of the sin you carry?
JULIET. I do; and bear the shame most patiently.
DUKE. I'll teach you how you shall arraign your conscience,
> And try your penitence, if it be sound
> Or hollowly put on.
JULIET. I'll gladly learn.
DUKE. Love you the man that wrong'd you?
JULIET. Yes, as I love the woman that wrong'd him.
DUKE. So then, it seems, your most offenceful act
> Was mutually committed.
JULIET. Mutually.
DUKE. Then was your sin of heavier kind than his.
JULIET. I do confess it, and repent it, father.
DUKE. 'Tis meet so, daughter: but lest you do repent
> As that the sin hath brought you to this shame,—
> Which sorrow is always toward ourselves, not Heaven,
> Showing we would not spare Heaven[102] as we love it,
> But as we stand in fear,—
JULIET. I do repent me as it is an evil,
> And take the shame with joy.
DUKE. There rest.[103]
> Your partner, as I hear, must die to-morrow,
> And I am going with instruction to him.—
> Grace go with you!

---

[101] *In* for *into*; the two being often used indiscriminately.

[102] Here, if the text be right, we have a rather bold ellipsis; the required sense being "*forbear to offend* Heaven," or spare Heaven the offence of our sin. A like expression, however, occurs in *Coriolanus*, i. 1, where Brutus the Tribune says of the hero, "Being moved, he will not *spare to gird* the gods"; that is, "will not spare the gods in his girding."

[103] There *remain*, there *stand firm*, or "keep yourself in that frame of mind."

DUKE. *Benedicite*! [*Exit.*]
JULIET. Must die to-morrow! O, injurious law,
    That respites me a life whose very comfort
    Is still a dying horror!
PROVOST. 'Tis pity of him. [*Exeunt.*]

SCENE IV.

A Room in ANGELO'*s House.*

[*Enter* ANGELO.]

ANGELO. When I would pray and think, I think and pray
    To several subjects.[104] Heaven hath my empty words;
    Whilst my invention, hearing not my tongue,
    Anchors on Isabel: Heaven in my mouth,
    As if I did but only chew his name;
    And in my heart the strong and swelling evil
    Of my conception. The state whereon I studied
    Is, like a good thing, being often read,
    Grown sere[105] and tedious; yea, my gravity,
    Wherein—let no man hear me—I take pride,
    Could I with boot change for an idle plume,
    Which the air beats for vain. O place! O form!
    How often dost thou with thy case, thy habit,
    Wrench awe from fools, and tie the wiser souls
    To thy false seeming![106] Blood, thou art blood:
    Let's write *good angel* on the devil's horn,
    'Tis not the devil's crest.[107]—

[*Enter* SERVANT.]

How now, who's there?

---

[104] *Several* in its old sense of *separate* or *different.* Repeatedly so.

[105] *Sere* is *dry, withered.* So in *Macbeth*, v. 3: "My way of life is fall'n into the *sere*, the yellow leaf." And in Spenser's *Shepherd's Calendar*, January:

    All so my lustful leafe is drie and *sere*,
    My timely buds with wailing all are wasted.

[106] Fools, those who judge only by the eye, are easily awed by spendour; and those who regard men as well as conditions are easily induced to love the appearance of virtue dignified by power and place.

[107] The meaning appears to be, though we write *good angel* on the Devil's horn, still it will not change his nature, nor be his proper crest; will not be emblematic of his real character.

SERVANT. One Isabel, a sister, desires access to you.
ANGELO. Teach her the way.

[*Exit* SERVANT.]

O Heavens!
Why does my blood thus muster to my heart,
Making both it unable for itself
And dispossessing all the other parts
Of necessary fitness?
So play the foolish throngs with one that swoons;
Come all to help him, and so stop the air
By which he should revive: and even so
The general,[108] subject to a well-wished king
Quit their own part, and in obsequious fondness
Crowd to his presence, where their untaught love
Must needs appear offence.—

[*Enter* ISABELLA.]

How now, fair maid?
ISABELLA. I am come to know your pleasure.
ANGELO. That you might know it, would much better please me
    Than to demand what 'tis. Your brother cannot live.
ISABELLA. Even so?—Heaven keep your Honour! [*Retiring.*]
ANGELO. Yet may he live awhile: and, it may be,
    As long as you or I: yet he must die.
ISABELLA. Under your sentence?
ANGELO. Yea.
ISABELLA. When? I beseech you? that in his reprieve,
    Longer or shorter, he may be so fitted
    That his soul sicken not.
ANGELO. Ha! Fie, these filthy vices! It were as good
    To pardon him that hath from nature stolen
    A man already made, as to remit
    Their saucy sweetness that do coin Heaven's image
    In stamps that are forbid; 'tis all as easy
    Falsely to take away a life true made
    As to put metal in restrained moulds
    To make a false one.[109]

---

[108] "The *general*" for what we sometimes call the *generality*, that is, the *multitude*. Shakespeare often thus uses an adjective with the sense of the plural substantive. So in *Hamlet*, i. 2: "The levies, the lists, and full proportions, are all made out of his *subject*."

[109] Meaning, probably, that murder is as easy as fornication; from which Angelo would infer that it is as wrong to pardon the latter as the former.

ISABELLA. 'Tis set down so in Heaven, but not in earth.
ANGELO. Say you so? then I shall pose you quickly.
    Which had you rather,—that the most just law
    Now took your brother's life; or, to redeem him,
    Give up your body to such sweet uncleanness
    As she that he hath stain'd?
ISABELLA. Sir, believe this,
    I had rather give my body than my soul.
ANGELO. I talk not of your soul; our compell'd sins
    Stand more for number than for account.
ISABELLA. How say you?
ANGELO. Nay, I'll not warrant that; for I can speak
    Against the thing I say. Answer to this;—
    I, now the voice of the recorded law,
    Pronounce a sentence on your brother's life:
    Might there not be a charity in sin,
    To save this brother's life?
ISABELLA. Please you to do't,
    I'll take it as a peril to my soul,[110]
    It is no sin at all, but charity.
ANGELO. Pleas'd you to do't at peril of your soul,
    Were equal poise of sin and charity.
ISABELLA. That I do beg his life, if it be sin,
    Heaven let me bear it! You granting of my suit,
    If that be sin, I'll make it my morn prayer
    To have it added to the faults of mine,
    And nothing of your answer.[111]
ANGELO. Nay, but hear me:
    Your sense pursues not mine: either you are ignorant
    Or seem so, craftily; and that's not good.
ISABELLA. Let me be ignorant, and in nothing good
    But graciously to know I am no better.
ANGELO. Thus wisdom wishes to appear most bright
    When it doth tax itself: as these black masks
    Proclaim an enshield[112] beauty ten times louder

---

[110] We should say, "I'll take it *on the* peril *of* my soul"; meaning, "I'll stake my soul upon it."

[111] Here, as often, *of is* equivalent to *in respect of. Answer* has the force of *responsibility.* "And be nothing in respect of which, or for which, you will have to answer."

[112] *Enshield* for *enshielded*; that is, covered or protected as with a shield. The Poet, as I have before noted, has many such shortened forms; as *hoist* for *hoisted*, *quit* for *quitted*, *frustrate* for *frustrated*, &c. And so in Bacon's Essay *Of Vicissitude of Things*: "Learning hath, lastly, its old age, when it waxeth dry and *exhaust.*"—In "these black masks," *these* is used *indefinitely*; that is, "the demonstrative pronoun for the prepositive article." This is an ancient and still current idiom of the language.

Than beauty could, displayed.—But mark me;
To be received plain, I'll speak more gross:
Your brother is to die.

ISABELLA. So.

ANGELO. And his offence is so, as it appears,
Accountant to the law upon that pain.

ISABELLA. True.

ANGELO. Admit no other way to save his life,—
As I subscribe not that, nor any other,—
But (in the loss of question) that you, his sister,[113]
Finding yourself desir'd of such a person,
Whose credit with the judge, or own great place,
Could fetch your brother from the manacles
Of the all-binding law; and that there were
No earthly mean to save him but that either
You must lay down the treasures of your body
To this suppos'd, or else to let him suffer;
What would you do?

ISABELLA. As much for my poor brother as myself:
That is, were I under the terms of death,
The impression of keen whips I'd wear as rubies,
And strip myself to death, as to a bed
That longing have been sick for, ere I'd yield
My body up to shame.

ANGELO. Then must
Your brother die.

ISABELLA. And 'twere the cheaper way:
Better it were a brother died at once
Than that a sister, by redeeming him,
Should die for ever.

ANGELO. Were not you, then, as cruel as the sentence
That you have slandered so?

ISABELLA. Ignomy[114] in ransom and free pardon
Are of two houses; lawful mercy
Is nothing kin to foul redemption.

ANGELO. You seem'd of late to make the law a tyrant;
And rather prov'd the sliding of your brother
A merriment than a vice.

---

[113] Here the order, according to the sense, is, "Admit no other way to save his life, but that you, his sister," &c. The meaning is somewhat perplexed and obscured by the intervening passages, which are all parenthetical.—"In the loss of question" means simply, as I take it, "in idle talk," or, as Mr. White well puts it," in the waste of words." The Poet repeatedly uses *question* thus for *talk* or *conversation.* The obscurity of the text is somewhat enhanced or thickened to us by this obsolete use of the word.

[114] *Ignomy is,* but a shortened form of *ignominy;* used several times by the Poet.

ISABELLA. O, pardon me, my lord! It oft falls out,
    To have what we would have, we speak not what we mean:
    I something do excuse the thing I hate
    For his advantage that I dearly love.
ANGELO. We are all frail.
ISABELLA. Else let my brother die,
    If not a federy, but only he,
    Owe, and succeed by weakness.[115]
ANGELO. Nay, women are frail too.
ISABELLA. Ay, as the glasses where they view themselves;
    Which are as easy broke as they make forms.
    Women!—Help Heaven! men their creation mar
    In profiting by them. Nay, call us ten times frail;
    For we are soft as our complexions are,
    And credulous to false prints.[116]
ANGELO. I think it well:
    And from this testimony of your own sex,—
    Since, I suppose, we are made to be no stronger
    Than faults may shake our frames,[117]—let me be bold;—
    I do arrest your words. Be that you are,
    That is, a woman; if you be more, you're none;
    If you be one,—as you are well express'd
    By all external warrants,—show it now
    By putting on the destin'd livery.
ISABELLA. I have no tongue but one: gentle, my lord,
    Let me intreat you, speak the former language.
ANGELO. Plainly conceive, I love you.
ISABELLA. My brother did love Juliet; and you tell me
    That he shall die for it.
ANGELO. He shall not, Isabel, if you give me love.
ISABELLA. I know your virtue hath a license in't,
    Which seems a little fouler than it is,
    To pluck on others.[118]

---

[115] *Fedary* is used by Shakespeare for *associate, partner,* or *confederate.*—*Owe,* as usual, is *own, have,* or *possess.*—*Succeed* is *follow* or *take after.*—So that the sense of the whole passage is, "If my brother alone, without a partner, owned and took after this weakness, then I would say, let him die." The odd use of *fedary, owe,* and *succeed* makes it obscure to modern ears.

[116] "Credulous to false prints" means apt to trust false shows and pretences, or to take the painting or "counterfeit presentment" of a virtue for the thing itself. Women are not alone in that.

[117] Old English, meaning, in modern phrase, "not made to be *so strong but that* faults may shake our frames." A somewhat similar expression occurs in *All's Well.*

[118] "To *pluck on* others" means, to pull or *draw* others into a disclosure of their hidden faults. Isabella cannot yet believe the man to be so bad as he talks, and thinks he is now assuming a vice in order to try what she is made of, or to draw her out.

ANGELO. Believe me, on mine Honour,
    My words express my purpose.
ISABELLA. Ha! little Honour to be much believed,
    And most pernicious purpose!—Seeming, seeming!—
    I will proclaim thee, Angelo; look for't:
    Sign me a present pardon for my brother
    Or, with an outstretch'd throat, I'll tell the world
    Aloud what man thou art.
ANGELO. Who will believe thee, Isabel?
    My unsoil'd name, th' austereness of my life,
    My vouch against you, and my place i' the state,
    Will so your accusation overweigh
    That you shall stifle in your own report,
    And smell of calumny. I have begun,
    And now I give my sensual race[119] the rein:
    Fit thy consent to my sharp appetite;
    Lay by all nicety and prolixious blushes,[120]
    That banish what they sue for: redeem thy brother
    By yielding up thy body to my will;
    Or else he must not only die the death,
    But thy unkindness shall his death draw out
    To lingering sufferance: answer me to-morrow,
    Or, by the affection that now guides me most,
    I'll prove a tyrant to him. As for you,
    Say what you can, my false o'erweighs your true. [*Exit.*]
ISABELLA. To whom should I complain? Did tell this,
    Who would believe me? O perilous mouths
    That bear in them one and the self-same tongue
    Either of condemnation or approof;[121]
    Bidding the law make court'sy to their will;
    Hooking both right and wrong to the appetite,
    To follow as it draws! I'll to my brother:
    Though he hath fallen by prompture of the blood,
    Yet hath he in him such a mind of honour,[122]
    That, had he twenty heads to tender down
    On twenty bloody blocks, he'd yield them up
    Before his sister should her body stoop

---

[119] *Race*, here, is *native bent* or *inborn aptitude*; like the Latin *indoles*. So again in *The Tempest*, i. 2: "But thy vile *race* had that in't which good natures could not abide to be with."

[120] "Prolixious blushes" are blushes that *put off* or *postpone* the conclusion; what Milton calls "sweet, reluctant, amorous delay."

[121] *Approof* is *approval* or *approbation*.

[122] "Mind of honour" for honourable mind, or mind full of noble thought. So the Poet has "mind of love" for loving mind, and other like phrases.

To such abhorr'd pollution.
Then, Isabel, live chaste, and, brother, die:
More than our brother is our chastity.
I'll tell him yet of Angelo's request,
And fit his mind to death, for his soul's rest. [*Exit.*]

ACT III.

SCENE I.

A Room in the Prison.

[*Enter the* DUKE *disguised as before*, CLAUDIO, *and the* PROVOST.]

DUKE. So, then you hope of pardon from Lord Angelo?
CLAUDIO. The miserable have no other medicine
    But only hope:
    I have hope to live, and am prepar'd to die.
DUKE. Be absolute for death; either death or life
    Shall thereby be the sweeter. Reason thus with life,—
    If I do lose thee, I do lose a thing
    That none but fools would keep: a breath thou art,
    Servile to all the skiey influences,
    That dost this habitation, where thou keep'st,[123]
    Hourly afflict; merely, thou art Death's Fool;[124]
    For him thou labour'st by thy flight to shun,
    And yet runn'st toward him still. Thou art not noble;
    For all the accommodations that thou bear'st
    Are nurs'd by baseness. Thou art by no means valiant;
    For thou dost fear the soft and tender fork
    Of a poor worm.[125] Thy best of rest is sleep,
    And that thou oft provok'st; yet grossly fear'st
    Thy death, which is no more. Thou art not thyself:
    For thou exist'st on many a thousand grains
    That issue out of dust. Happy thou art not;

---

[123] *Keep*, again, for *dwell.* See page 27, note 37.
[124] *Merely* in the sense of *absolutely.* Often so.—Death and his Fool were famous personages in the old Moral-plays. Douce had an old wood-cut, one of a series representing the Dance of Death, in which the Fool was engaged in combat with Death, and buffetting him with a bladder filled with peas or small pebbles. The moral of those performances was, that the Fool, after struggling against his adversary, at last became his victim.
[125] *Worm* is put for any creeping thing, *snake*, or *serpent.* Shakespeare seems to have held the current notion, that a serpent wounds with his *tongue*, and that this is *forked.*

For what thou hast not, still thou striv'st to get;
And what thou hast, forgett'st. Thou art not certain;
For thy complexion shifts to strange affects,[126]
After the moon. If thou art rich, thou art poor;
For, like an ass whose back with ingots bows,
Thou bear'st thy heavy riches but a journey,
And death unloads thee. Friend hast thou none;
For thine own bowels, which do call thee sire,
The mere effusion of thy proper loins,
Do curse the gout, serpigo,[127] and the rheum,
For ending thee no sooner. Thou hast nor youth nor age,
But, as it were, an after-dinner's sleep,
Dreaming on both: for all thy blessed youth
Becomes as aged, and doth beg the alms
Of palsied eld;[128] and when thou art old and rich
Thou hast neither heat, affection, limb, nor beauty,
To make thy riches pleasant. What's yet in this
That bears the name of life? Yet in this life
Lie hid more thousand deaths: yet death we fear,
That makes these odds all even.
CLAUDIO. I humbly thank you.
To sue to live,[129] I find I seek to die;
And, seeking death, find life. Let it come on.
ISABELLA. [*Within.*] What, ho! Peace here; grace and good company!
PROVOST. Who's there? come in: the wish deserves a welcome.
DUKE. Dear son, ere long I'll visit you again.
CLAUDIO. Most holy sir, I thank you.

[*Enter* ISABELLA.]

ISABELLA. My business is a word or two with Claudio.
PROVOST. And very welcome.—Look, signior, here's your sister.
DUKE. Provost, a word with you.
PROVOST. As many as you please.
DUKE. Bring me to hear them speak, where I may be conceal'd.

---

[126] The Poet has *affects* repeatedly for *affections.*—*Complexion* is here used in its old sense of *natural texture* or *grain*; very much as *temperament* is now.

[127] The *serpigo* is a sort of tetter or leprous eruption.

[128] "Palsied eld" is tremulous old age.—This strain of moralizing may be rendered something thus: "In youth, which is or ought to be the happiest time, man commonly lacks the means of what he considers enjoyment; he has to beg alms of hoary avarice; and, being niggardly supplied, he *becomes as aged*, or looks, like an old man, on happiness beyond his reach."

[129] *To sue* is another instance of the infinitive used gerundively, or like the Latin *gerund*, and so is equivalent to *in* or *by suing.* So again, a little further on, "*To cleave* a heart"; that is, *by cleaving.*

[*Exeunt the* DUKE, *and* PROVOST.]

CLAUDIO. Now, sister, what's the comfort?
ISABELLA. Why,
    As all comforts are; most good, most good, in deed:
    Lord Angelo, having affairs to Heaven,
    Intends you for his swift ambassador,
    Where you shall be an everlasting leiger:[130]
    Therefore, your best appointment[131] make with speed;
    To-morrow you set on.
CLAUDIO. Is there no remedy?
ISABELLA. None, but such remedy as, to save a head,
    To cleave a heart in twain.
CLAUDIO. But is there any?
ISABELLA. Yes, brother, you may live:
    There is a devilish mercy in the judge,
    If you'll implore it, that will free your life,
    But fetter you till death.
CLAUDIO. Perpetual durance?
ISABELLA. Ay, just; perpetual durance,—a restraint,
    Though all the world's vastidity[132] you had,
    To a determin'd scope.[133]
CLAUDIO. But in what nature?
ISABELLA. In such a one as, you consenting to't,
    Would bark your Honour from that trunk you bear,
    And leave you naked.
CLAUDIO. Let me know the point.
ISABELLA. O, I do fear thee, Claudio; and I quake,
    Lest thou a feverous life shouldst entertain,
    And six or seven winters more respect
    Than a perpetual Honour. Dar'st thou die?
    The sense of death is most in apprehension;
    And the poor beetle that we tread upon
    In corporal sufferance finds a pang as great
    As when a giant dies.[134]

---

[130] A *lieger* is a *resident*, or minister residing at a foreign court.

[131] *Appointment* for *preparation* or *outfit*. Still used thus in military language; as a *well-appointed* army, meaning an army well equipped or furnished.

[132] *Vastidity* for *vastness*; the only instance of the word in Shakespeare.

[133] "Shutting you up in a perpetual sense and shame of your own ignominy." *Determined* in its old sense of *limited, confined,* or *narrow;* literally, fenced-in with *terms,* that is, *bounds.*

[134] This is apt to be misunderstood, though probably not quite true in any sense. The meaning is, that the apprehension of death is the chief pain, and that a giant feels no more pain in death itself than a beetle.

CLAUDIO. Why give you me this shame?
  Think you I can a resolution fetch
  From flowery tenderness?[135] If I must die,
  I will encounter darkness as a bride
  And hug it in mine arms.
ISABELLA. There spake my brother; there my father's grave
  Did utter forth a voice! Yes, thou must die:
  Thou art too noble to conserve a life
  In base appliances. This outward-sainted deputy—
  Whose settled visage and deliberate word
  Nips youth i' the head, and follies doth enew
  As falcon doth the fowl[136]—is yet a devil;
  His filth within being cast, he would appear
  A pond as deep as hell.
CLAUDIO. The precise Angelo?
ISABELLA. O, 'tis the cunning livery of hell
  The damned'st body to invest and cover
  In precise guards![137] Dost thou think, Claudio,
  If I would yield him my virginity
  Thou mightst be freed?
CLAUDIO. O Heavens! it cannot be.

---

[135] I am not quite sure as to the meaning here; but it seems to be, "Do you think me so effeminate in soul as to be capable of an unmanly resolution?" or, "such a milksop as to quail and collapse at the prospect of death?" Perhaps the sentence should be imperative, thus: "Think you, I can a resolution fetch from flowery tenderness." So Heath proposes; and explains, "Do me the justice to think that I am able to draw a resolution even from this tenderness of my youth, which is commonly found to be less easily reconciled to so sudden and harsh a fate."

[136] *Enew*, from the French *eneau*, was a technical term in aquatic falconry, and was used, to denote the act of forcing the fowl back to the water, as her only sure refuge from the souse of the hawk. The best, indeed the only, explanation of the word that I have met with is in *The Edinburgh Review*, October, 1872. I condense a part of the matter: When a flight at water fowl was in hand, the falconer whistled off his hawk at some distance from the spot where the duck or mallard, the heron or crane, was known to be. The hawk having reached a tolerable height, the falconer, with his dogs and assistants, "made in" upon the fowl, forcing its flight, if possible, in the direction of the land. This was termed *landing* the fowl, a vital point in aquatic falconry. For, in order that the hawk might stoop with effect, it was necessary to have solid ground immediately beneath; else the hawk might stoop in vain, the fowl taking refuge in diving. The fowl having been thus landed, the hawk would stoop swiftly on its prey; while the former, to avoid the fatal stroke, would instinctively make for the water again. In this case the fowl was said to be *enewed*; that is, forced back to the water, from which it had to be driven afresh and landed, before the hawk could stoop and seize its prey. The fowl was often enewed several times before it was landed effectively enough for the final swoop. From this technical use, the word came to be applied in the more general sense of to *drive back* and pursue *relentlessly*. It would thus be naturally used of a course of extreme and vindictive severity.

[137] *Guards* was in common use for the *facings* and *trimmings* of the dress. Both the guards and the wearer of them are called *priestly*, not because Angelo is a priest, but because, in his dress and manners, he has "stolen the livery of Heaven to serve the Devil in."

ISABELLA. Yes, he would give it thee, from this rank offence,
 So to offend him still.[138] This night's the time
 That I should do what I abhor to name,
 Or else thou diest to-morrow.
CLAUDIO. Thou shalt not do't.
ISABELLA. O, were it but my life,
 I'd throw it down for your deliverance
 As frankly as a pin.
CLAUDIO. Thanks, dear Isabel.
ISABELLA. Be ready, Claudio, for your death to-morrow.
CLAUDIO. Yes.—Has he affections in him
 That thus can make him bite the law by the nose
 When he would force it? Sure it is no sin;
 Or of the deadly seven it is the least.
ISABELLA. Which is the least?
CLAUDIO. If it were damnable, he, being so wise,
 Why would he for the momentary trick
 Be perdurably fined?—O Isabel!
ISABELLA. What says my brother?
CLAUDIO. Death is a fearful thing.
ISABELLA. And shamed life a hateful.
CLAUDIO. Ay, but to die, and go we know not where;
 To lie in cold obstruction, and to rot;
 This sensible warm motion to become
 A kneaded clod; and the delighted[139] spirit
 To bathe in fiery floods or to reside
 In thrilling regions of thick-ribbed ice;[140]
 To be imprison'd in the viewless winds,
 And blown with restless violence round about
 The pendent world; or to be worse than worst
 Of those that lawless and incertain thought
 Imagine howling!—'tis too horrible!

---

[138] The meaning seems to be, "So gross an offence having once been committed by me, you might thenceforth persist in sinning with safety." Her possession of such a secret would naturally assure him of impunity, however often he might be guilty in the same kind.

[139] A rather singular use of *delighted*; involving a sort of inverted prolepsis; and meaning the spirit that *has been delighted*, or *formed to* and *steeped in delight*; the word *delight* being taken in the sense of the Latin *deliciæ*.

[140] Milton no doubt had this passage in mind when he wrote the lines, 600-603, in *Paradise Lost*, Book ii.:

 From beds of raging fire, to starve in ice
 Their soft ethereal warmth, and there to pine
 Immovable-infix'd, and frozen round,
 Periods of time; thence hurried back to fire.

    The weariest and most loathed worldly life
    That age, ache, penury, and imprisonment
    Can lay on nature is a paradise
    To what we fear of death.
ISABELLA. Alas, alas!
CLAUDIO. Sweet sister, let me live:
    What sin you do to save a brother's life
    Nature dispenses with the deed so far
    That it becomes a virtue.
ISABELLA. O you beast!
    O faithless coward! O dishonest wretch!
    Wilt thou be made a man out of my vice?
    Is't not a kind of incest to take life
    From thine own sister's shame? What should I think?
    Heaven shield my mother play'd my father fair!
    For such a warped slip of wilderness[141]
    Ne'er issued from his blood. Take my defiance;[142]
    Die; perish! might but my bending down
    Reprieve thee from thy fate, it should proceed:
    I'll pray a thousand prayers for thy death,—
    No word to save thee.
CLAUDIO. Nay, hear me, Isabel.
ISABELLA. O fie, fie, fie!
    Thy sin's not accidental, but a trade:
    Mercy to thee would prove itself a bawd:
    'Tis best that thou diest quickly. [*Going.*]
CLAUDIO. O, hear me, Isabella.

    [*Re-enter the* DUKE.]

DUKE. Vouchsafe a word, young sister, but one word.
ISABELLA. What is your will?
DUKE. Might you dispense with your leisure,[143] I would by and by
    have some speech with you: the satisfaction I would require is
    likewise your own benefit.
ISABELLA. I have no superfluous leisure; my stay must be stolen out
    of other affairs; but I will attend you awhile.
DUKE. [*Aside to* CLAUDIO.] Son, I have overheard what hath passed
    between you and your sister. Angelo had never the purpose to

---

[141] Such a *wild* slip; that is, not of the true stock or blood; *spurious. Wilderness* for *wildness*, simply.

[142] *Defiance* in the sense it bore as a legal term, *refusal*. So to *forsake* is one of the old senses of to *defy*.

[143] To *dispense with* a thing, in one of its senses, is to *do without* it, to *spare* it. And such appears to be the meaning here.

corrupt her; only he hath made an assay of her virtue to practise his judgment with the disposition of natures; she, having the truth of Honour in her, hath made him that gracious denial which he is most glad to receive: I am confessor to Angelo, and I know this to be true; therefore prepare yourself to death: do not qualify[144] your resolution with hopes that are fallible: to-morrow you must die; go to your knees and make ready.

CLAUDIO. Let me ask my sister pardon. I am so out of love with life that I will sue to be rid of it.

DUKE. Hold you there:[145] farewell.

[*Exit* CLAUDIO.]

—Provost, a word with you.

[*Re-enter the* PROVOST.]

PROVOST. What's your will, father?

DUKE. That, now you are come, you will be gone. Leave me a while with the maid; my mind promises with my habit no loss shall touch her by my company.

PROVOST. In good time.[146] [*Exit.*]

DUKE. The hand that hath made you fair hath made you good; the goodness that is cheap in beauty makes beauty brief in goodness;[147] but grace, being the soul of your complexion, shall keep the body of it ever fair. The assault that Angelo hath made to you, fortune hath conveyed to my understanding; and, but that frailty hath examples for his falling, I should wonder at Angelo. How will you do to content this substitute, and to save your brother?

ISABELLA. I am now going to resolve him.[148] I had rather my brother die by the law than my son should be unlawfully born. But, O, how much is the good Duke deceived in Angelo! If ever he return, and I can speak to him, I will open my lips in vain, or discover his government.

---

[144] *Qualify* in the sense of *abate*, *weaken*, or *dilute*. To be entertaining unsure hopes of life would naturally unsinew his resolution to meet death firmly. *Qualify* was often used thus.

[145] That is, *continue in* that *mind*. So *there rest*, used before.

[146] Meaning, *so be it*, or *very well*: like the French *a la bonne heure*.

[147] I do not well understand this. Does it mean, "she who, in her pride or confidence of beauty, holds virtue in light esteem, will easily part with her virtue"? That sense, I think, may fairly come from the words. In *Hamlet*, iii. 1, we have, "The power of beauty will sooner transform honesty from what it is to a bawd, than the force of honesty can translate beauty into his likeness."

[148] To *inform*, *assure*, or *certify* him. So the Poet often uses *resolve*.

DUKE. That shall not be much amiss: yet, as the matter now stands, he will avoid your accusation,—he made trial of you only.— Therefore fasten your ear on my advisings: to the love I have in doing good a remedy presents itself. I do make myself believe that you may most uprighteously do a poor wronged lady a merited benefit; redeem your brother from the angry law; do no stain to your own gracious person; and much please the absent Duke, if peradventure he shall ever return to have hearing of this business.

ISABELLA. Let me hear you speak further; I have spirit to do anything that appears not foul in the truth of my spirit.

DUKE. Virtue is bold, and goodness never fearful. Have you not heard speak of Mariana, the sister of Frederick, the great soldier who miscarried at sea?

ISABELLA. I have heard of the lady, and good words went with her name.

DUKE. She should this Angelo have married; was affianced to her by oath, and the nuptial appointed: between which time of the contract and limit of the solemnity her brother Frederick was wrecked at sea, having in that perished vessel the dowry of his sister. But mark how heavily this befell to the poor gentlewoman: there she lost a noble and renowned brother, in his love toward her ever most kind and natural; with him the portion and sinew of her fortune, her marriage-dowry; with both, her combinate[149] husband, this well-seeming Angelo.

ISABELLA. Can this be so? Did Angelo so leave her?

DUKE. Left her in her tears, and dried not one of them with his comfort; swallowed his vows whole, pretending, in her, discoveries of dishonour; in few, bestow'd her on her own lamentation, which she yet wears for his sake; and he, a marble to her tears, is washed with them, but relents not.

ISABELLA. What a merit were it in death to take this poor maid from the world! What corruption in this life that it will let this man live!—But how out of this can she avail?

DUKE. It is a rupture that you may easily heal; and the cure of it not only saves your brother, but keeps you from dishonour in doing it.

ISABELLA. Show me how, good father.

DUKE. This forenamed maid hath yet in her the continuance of her first affection; his unjust unkindness, that in all reason should have quenched her love, hath, like an impediment in the current, made it more violent and unruly. Go you to Angelo; answer his requiring with a plausible obedience; agree with his demands to the point:

---

[149] *Combinate* is *contracted* or *betrothed.* Rose, in his translation of *Orlando Furioso,* notes the "close and whimsical relation there often is between English and Italian idiom"; and adds, "Thus every Italian scholar understands 'her *combinate* husband' to mean her husband *elect.*"

only refer yourself[150] to this advantage,—first, that your stay with
him may not be long; that the time may have all shadow and
silence in it; and the place answer to convenience: this being
granted in course, and now follows all. We shall advise this
wronged maid to stead up your appointment, go in your place; if
the encounter acknowledge itself hereafter, it may compel him to
her recompense: and here, by this, is your brother saved, your
Honour untainted, the poor Mariana advantaged, and the corrupt
deputy scaled. The maid will I frame and make fit for his attempt.
If you think well to carry this as you may, the doubleness of the
benefit defends the deceit from reproof. What think you of it?

ISABELLA. The image of it gives me content already; and I trust it
will grow to a most prosperous perfection.

DUKE. It lies much in your holding up. Haste you speedily to Angelo;
if for this night he entreat you to his bed, give him promise of
satisfaction. I will presently to Saint Luke's; there, at the moated
grange,[151] resides this dejected Mariana. At that place call upon
me; and despatch with Angelo, that it may be quickly.

ISABELLA. I thank you for this comfort. Fare you well, good father.
[*Exeunt severally.*]

SCENE II.

The Street before the Prison.

[*Enter, on one side, the* DUKE *disguised as before; on the other,*
ELBOW, POMPEY *and* OFFICERS *with* POMPEY.]

ELBOW. Nay, if there be no remedy for it, but that you will needs buy
and sell men and women like beasts, we shall have all the world
drink brown and white bastard.[152]

DUKE. O Heavens! what stuff is here?

POMPEY. 'Twas never merry world since, of two usuries, the merriest
was put down, and the worser allowed by order of law a furred
gown to keep him warm; and furred with fox on lamb-skins too, to
signify that craft, being richer than innocency, stands for the
facing.

ELBOW. Come your way, sir.—Bless you, good father friar.

---

[150] "Refer yourself" here means *have recourse*, or *betake* yourself.

[151] A *grange* was properly a farm-house attached to a monastery, as here to the
monastery of Saint Luke's; but the word came to be used of any sequestered and lonely
house. Some granges were important enough to be *moated*, for defence.

[152] *Bastard* was the name of a sweetish wine; "approaching," says Dyce, "to the
muscadel in flavour, and perhaps made from a *bastard* species of muscadine grape."

DUKE. And you, good brother father.[153] What offence hath this man made you, sir?

ELBOW. Marry, sir, he hath offended the law; and, sir, we take him to be a thief too, sir; for we have found upon him, sir, a strange picklock, which we have sent to the deputy.

DUKE. Fie, sirrah, fie! a bawd, a wicked bawd!
The evil that thou causest to be done,
That is thy means to live. Do thou but think
What 'tis to cram a maw or clothe a back
From such a filthy vice: say to thyself,—
From their abominable and beastly touches
I drink, I eat, array myself, and live.
Canst thou believe thy living is a life,
So stinkingly depending? Go mend, go mend.

POMPEY. Indeed, it does stink in some sort, sir; but yet, sir, I would prove—

DUKE. Nay, if the devil have given thee proofs for sin,
Thou wilt prove his.—Take him to prison, officer;
Correction and instruction must both work
Ere this rude beast will profit.

ELBOW. He must before the deputy, sir; he has given him warning:
The deputy cannot abide a whoremaster: if he be a whoremaster,
and comes before him, he were as good go a mile on his errand.

DUKE. That we were all, as some would seem to be,
Free from our faults, as faults from seeming free!

ELBOW. His neck will come to your waist,—a cord,[154] sir.

POMPEY. I spy comfort; I cry bail! Here's a gentleman, and a friend of mine.

[*Enter* LUCIO.]

LUCIO. How now, noble Pompey? What, at the wheels of Cæsar! Art thou led in triumph? What, is there none of Pygmalion's images,[155] newly made woman, to be had now, for putting the hand in the pocket and extracting it clutched? What reply, ha? What say'st thou to this tune, matter, and method? Is't not drowned i' the last rain, ha? What say'st thou to't? Is the world as it was, man? Which

---

[153] The Duke sportively calls him *brother father* in return for his address, *father friar*, which means, literally, *father brother.*

[154] "His neck will come *to be like*" or in the condition of, "your waist"; alluding to the rope with which the Duke is girded as a part of his disguise.

[155] Pygmalion was something of an artist: he made an ivory image of a maiden, and wrought it to such a pitch of beauty, that he himself fell dead in love with it, and then took on so badly, that at his prayer the image became alive; and thereupon he made her his wife.

is the way? Is it sad, and few words? or how? The trick of it?

DUKE. Still thus, and thus! still worse!

LUCIO. How doth my dear morsel, thy mistress? Procures she still, ha?

POMPEY. Troth, sir, she hath eaten up all her beef, and she is herself in the tub.[156]

LUCIO. Why, 'tis good: it is the right of it: it must be so: ever your fresh whore and your powdered bawd—an unshunned consequence; it must be so. Art going to prison, Pompey?

POMPEY. Yes, faith, sir.

LUCIO. Why, 'tis not amiss, Pompey. Farewell; go, say I sent thee thither. For debt, Pompey? or how?

ELBOW. For being a bawd, for being a bawd.

LUCIO. Well, then, imprison him: if imprisonment be the due of a bawd, why, 'tis his right: bawd is he doubtless, and of antiquity, too: bawd-born.—Farewell, good Pompey. Commend me to the prison, Pompey. You will turn good husband now, Pompey; you will keep the house.[157]

POMPEY. I hope, sir, your good worship will be my bail.

LUCIO. No, indeed, will I not, Pompey; it is not the wear.[158] I will pray, Pompey, to increase your bondage: if you take it not patiently, why, your mettle is the more. Adieu, trusty Pompey.— Bless you, friar.

DUKE. And you.

LUCIO. Does Bridget paint still, Pompey, ha?

ELBOW. Come your ways, sir; come.

POMPEY. You will not bail me then, sir?

LUCIO. Then, Pompey, nor now.—What news abroad, friar? what news?

ELBOW. Come your ways, sir; come.

LUCIO. Go,—to kennel, Pompey, go.

[*Exeunt* ELBOW, *and* Officers with POMPEY.]

—What news, friar, of the Duke?

DUKE. I know none. Can you tell me of any?

LUCIO. Some say he is with the Emperor of Russia; other some, he is in Rome: but where is he, think you?

DUKE. I know not where; but wheresoever, I wish him well.

LUCIO. It was a mad fantastical trick of him to steal from the state and

---

[156] Alluding to what was called the *powdering-tub* or sweating-tub, much used in curing the *lues venera.*—*Unshunn'd*, in the next speech, is *unshunable* or *inevitable.* The Poet has many instances of such usage.

[157] Alluding to the primitive meaning of *husband, house-band*; that is, *keeper* of the house, or *band* that held it together.

[158] *Wear* is *fashion*; used thus by the Poet several times.

usurp the beggary he was never born to. Lord Angelo dukes it well in his absence; he puts transgression to't.

DUKE. He does well in't.

LUCIO. A little more lenity to lechery would do no harm in him: something too crabbed that way, friar.

DUKE. It is too general a vice, and severity must cure it.

LUCIO. Yes, in good sooth, the vice is of a great kindred; it is well allied: but it is impossible to extirp it quite, friar, till eating and drinking be put down. They say this Angelo was not made by man and woman after this downright way of creation: is it true, think you?

DUKE. How should he be made, then?

LUCIO. Some report a sea-maid spawned him; some, that he was begot between two stock-fishes. But it is certain that when he makes water, his urine is congealed ice; that I know to be true. And he is a motion[159] ungenerative; that's infallible.

DUKE. You are pleasant, sir, and speak apace.

LUCIO. Why, what a ruthless thing is this in him, for the rebellion of a codpiece to take away the life of a man! Would the Duke that is absent have done this? Ere he would have hanged a man for the getting a hundred bastards, he would have paid for the nursing a thousand. He had some feeling of the sport; he knew the service, and that instructed him to mercy.

DUKE. I never heard the absent Duke much detected[160] for women; he was not inclined that way.

LUCIO. O, sir, you are deceived.

DUKE. 'Tis not possible.

LUCIO. Who, not the Duke? yes, your beggar of fifty;—and his use was to put a ducat in her clack-dish:[161] the Duke had crotchets in him. He would be drunk too: that let me inform you.

DUKE. You do him wrong, surely.

LUCIO. Sir, I was an inward[162] of his. A shy fellow was the Duke: and I believe I know the cause of his withdrawing.

DUKE. What, I pr'ythee, might be the cause?

LUCIO. No,—pardon;—'tis a secret must be locked within the teeth and the lips: but this I can let you understand,—the greater file[163] of the subject held the Duke to be wise.

DUKE. Wise? why, no question but he was.

---

[159] *Motion* was used continually for *puppet*.

[160] *Detected*, here, probably means *discovered*. The passage is commonly explained "*suspected* or *accused* in the matter of women."

[161] A wooden dish or box, formerly carried by beggars: it had a movable cover, which they *clacked* or clattered, to attract notice; and in it they received the alms.

[162] An *inward* is an *intimate*, or a *familiar friend*.

[163] "The greater *file*" is the longer *list*; that is, the larger number.

LUCIO. A very superficial, ignorant, unweighing fellow.

DUKE. Either this is envy[164] in you, folly, or mistaking; the very stream of his life, and the business he hath helmed[165] must, upon a warranted need, give him a better proclamation. Let him be but testimonied in his own bringings forth, and he shall appear to the envious a scholar, a statesman, and a soldier. Therefore you speak unskilfully; or, if your knowledge be more, it is much darkened in your malice.

LUCIO. Sir, I know him, and I love him.

DUKE. Love talks with better knowledge, and knowledge with dearer love.

LUCIO. Come, sir, I know what I know.

DUKE. I can hardly believe that, since you know not what you speak. But, if ever the Duke return,—as our prayers are he may,—let me desire you to make your answer before him. If it be honest you have spoke, you have courage to maintain it: I am bound to call upon you; and, I pray you, your name?

LUCIO. Sir, my name is Lucio; well known to the Duke.

DUKE. He shall know you better, sir, if I may live to report you.

LUCIO. I fear you not.

DUKE. O, you hope the Duke will return no more; or you imagine me too unhurtful an opposite.[166] But, indeed, I can do you little harm: you'll forswear this again.

LUCIO. I'll be hanged first! thou art deceived in me, friar. But no more of this. Canst thou tell if Claudio die to-morrow or no?

DUKE. Why should he die, sir?

LUCIO. Why? for filling a bottle with a tun-dish. I would the Duke we talk of were returned again: this ungenitured agent[167] will unpeople the province with continency; sparrows must not build in his house-eaves because they are lecherous. The Duke yet would have dark deeds darkly answered; he would never bring them to light: would he were returned! Marry, this Claudio is condemned for untrussing.[168] Farewell, good friar; I pr'ythee pray for me. The Duke, I say to thee again, would eat mutton on Fridays.[169] He's not past it; yet, and, I say to thee, he would mouth with a beggar though she smelt brown bread and garlic. Say that I said so.

---

[164] *Envy*, again, for *malice.* Also, a little after, *envious* for *malicious.* See page 29, note 41.

[165] *Helmed* is *guided*, or *steered through.*

[166] *Opposite* is constantly used by Shakespeare for *opponent.*

[167] *Ungenitured* is *unfathered*, not begotten in the ordinary way.—*Tundish*, two lines before, is an old word for *tunnel* or *funnel.*

[168] *Untrussing* was used of *untying* the tagged laces which, instead of buttons, fastened the hose or breeches to the doublet.

[169] An equivoque; *mutton* being a cant term for a *loose woman.* Of course, the Duke, being a good Catholic, would abstain from meat on Fridays, or pretend to do so.

Farewell. [*Exit.*]

DUKE. No might nor greatness in mortality
    Can censure 'scape; back-wounding calumny
    The whitest virtue strikes. What king so strong
    Can tie the gall up in the slanderous tongue?
    But who comes here?

[*Enter* ESCALUS, *the* Provost, *and* OFFICERS *with* MISTRESS
OVERDONE.]

ESCALUS. Go; away with her to prison!

MISTRESS OVERDONE. Good my lord,[170] be good to me; your
Honour is accounted a merciful man; good my lord.

ESCALUS. Double and treble admonition, and still forfeit in the same
kind? This would make mercy swear and play the tyrant.

PROVOST. A bawd of eleven years' continuance, may it please your
Honour.

MISTRESS OVERDONE. My lord, this is one Lucio's information
against me: Mistress Kate Keep-down was with child by him in the
Duke's time; he promised her marriage: his child is a year and a
quarter old come Philip and Jacob:[171] I have kept it myself; and see
how he goes about to abuse me.

ESCALUS. That fellow is a fellow of much license:—let him be called
before us.—Away with her to prison. Go to; no more words.

[*Exeunt* OFFICERS *with* MISTRESS OVERDONE.]

—Provost, my brother Angelo will not be altered, Claudio must die
to-morrow: let him be furnished with divines, and have all
charitable preparation: if my brother wrought by my pity it should
not be so with him.

PROVOST. So please you, this friar hath been with him, and advised
him for the entertainment of death.

ESCALUS. Good even, good father.

DUKE. Bliss and goodness on you!

ESCALUS. Of whence are you?

DUKE. Not of this country, though my chance is now
    To use it for my time: I am a brother
    Of gracious order, late come from the see
    In special business from his holiness.

ESCALUS. What news abroad i' the world?

---

[170] "Good my lord" for "my good lord." Such inversions occur continually in these
plays. So we have "dear my sister," "gentle my brother," "sweet my coz," "gracious my
mother," and many others.

[171] That is, the feast of the Apostles Philip and James, May I.

DUKE. None, but that there is so great a fever on goodness, that the
dissolution of it must cure it: novelty is only in request; and as it is
as dangerous to be aged in any kind of course as it is virtuous to be
constant in any undertaking. There is scarce truth enough alive to
make societies secure; but security enough to make fellowships
accursed:[172]—much upon this riddle runs the wisdom of the world.
This news is old enough, yet it is every day's news. I pray you, sir,
of what disposition was the Duke?

ESCALUS. One that, above all other strifes, contended especially to
know himself.

DUKE. What pleasure was he given to?

ESCALUS. Rather rejoicing to see another merry, than merry at
anything which professed to make him rejoice: a gentleman of all
temperance. But leave we him to his events, with a prayer they
may prove prosperous; and let me desire to know how you find
Claudio prepared. I am made to understand that you have lent him
visitation.

DUKE. He professes to have received no sinister measure from his
judge, but most willingly humbles himself to the determination of
justice: yet had he framed to himself, by the instruction of his
frailty, many deceiving promises of life; which I, by my good
leisure, have discredited to him, and now he is resolved to die.[173]

ESCALUS. You have paid the Heavens your function,[174] and the
prisoner the very debt of your calling. I have laboured for the poor
gentleman to the extremest shore of my modesty; but my brother
justice have I found so severe that he hath forced me to tell him he
is indeed Justice.[175]

DUKE. If his own life answer the straitness of his proceeding, it shall
become him well: wherein if he chance to fail, he hath sentenced
himself.

ESCALUS. I am going to visit the prisoner.
Fare you well.

DUKE. Peace be with you!—

[*Exeunt* ESCALUS *and* PROVOST.]

He who the sword of Heaven will bear
Should be as holy as severe;

---

[172] Alluding to those legal *securities* which fellowship leads men to enter into for
each other. Perhaps Shakespeare had in mind Proverbs, xi. 15: "He that hateth *suretiship*
is *sure.*"

[173] Is *satisfied*, or has *made up his mind*, to die. See *The Winter's Tale*, v. 3, note 6.

[174] To *pay a function* means the same as to *discharge a duty.*

[175] Probably spoken with an eye to the old maxim, *Summum jus summa injuria.* "A
rigid adherence to the letter of justice kills its spirit."

Pattern in himself to know,
Grace to stand, and virtue go;[176]
More nor less to others paying
Than by self-offences weighing.
Shame to him whose cruel striking
Kills for faults of his own liking!
Twice treble shame on Angelo,
To weed my vice,[177] and let his grow!
O, what may man within him hide,
Though angel on the outward side!
How may likeness, made in crimes,—
Make a practice on the times,—
To draw with idle spiders' strings
Most pond'rous and substantial things![178]
Craft against vice I must apply;
With Angelo to-night shall lie
His old betrothed but despis'd;
So disguise shall, by the disguised,
Pay with falsehood false exacting,[179]
And perform an old contracting. [*Exit.*]

---

[176] "Grace to stand, and virtue *to* go," is the meaning. Perhaps it were better to read, as Coleridge suggested, "Grace to stand, virtue to go."

[177] Referring, probably, to what the Duke has already said of himself, in i. 4: "Sith 'twas my fault to give the people scope."

[178] This whole soliloquy is rather un-Shakespearian, to say the least, and here it is somewhat obscure. But *likeness* probably means the same here as what the Poet elsewhere calls *virtuous-seeming*; that is, counterfeit semblance. So that the meaning comes something thus: "How may hypocrisy, by beguiling and hoodwinking the time, manage, in a course of criminal action, to draw to itself the greatest advantages by invisible threads."

[179] Here *disguise* is put for a *disguised person*, and refers to Mariana, who is to cause herself to be falsely taken for Isabella; and *the disguised* is Angelo, who is practising wickedness under the guise of sanctity. Thus Mariana is, with her *honest* falsehood, to pay off Angelo's "false exacting," that is, the sacrifice which he treacherously extorts from Isabella. It is hardly needful to say that perspicuity is here sacrificed to a jingle of words.

ACT IV.

SCENE I.

Before MARIANA's *House.*

[MARIANA *discovered sitting*; *a* BOY *singing.*]

SONG.

> *Take, O, take those lips away,*
>   *That so sweetly were forsworn;*
> *And those eyes, the break of day,*
>   *Lights that do mislead the morn:*
> *But my kisses bring again*
>   *Bring again;*
> *Seals of love, but seal'd in vain,*
>   *Sealed in vain.*[180]

MARIANA. Break off thy song, and haste thee quick away;
  Here comes a man of comfort, whose advice
  Hath often still'd my brawling discontent.—[*Exit* BOY.]

[*Enter the* DUKE *disguised as before.*]

  I cry you mercy,[181] sir; and well could wish
  You had not found me here so musical:
  Let me excuse me, and believe me so,—
  My mirth it much displeas'd, but pleas'd my woe.[182]
DUKE. 'Tis good: though music oft hath such a charm

---

[180] To this stanza, which I am sure none but Shakespeare could have written, is commonly appended another, which I am equally sure Shakespeare did not write, and which appeared first in Fletcher's *Bloody Brother.* The two stanzas are there printed together as forming one song; though, as Mr. White justly remarks, "the stanza added in that play is palpably addressed to a woman, while this is clearly addressed to a man." However, I here subjoin the other stanza, that the reader may compare them for himself:

> Hide, O, hide those hills of snow,
>   Which thy frozen bosom bears,
> On whose tops the pinks that grow
>   Are of those that April wears!
> But first set my poor heart free,
> Bound in those icy chains by thee.

[181] "I cry you mercy" is the old phrase for "I ask your pardon."
[182] "The music was far from making me merry, but it assuaged my sorrow."

To make bad good and good provoke to harm.
I pray you, tell me hath anybody inquired for me here to-day?
much upon this time have I promised here to meet.[183]

MARIANA. You have not been inquired after: I have sat here all day.

[*Enter* ISABELLA.]

DUKE. I do constantly believe you.—The time is come even now. I
    shall crave your forbearance a little: may be I will call upon you
    anon, for some advantage to yourself.
MARIANA. I am always bound to you. [*Exit.*]
DUKE. Very well met, and welcome.
What is the news from this good deputy?
ISABELLA. He hath a garden circummured[184] with brick,
    Whose western side is with a vineyard back'd;
    And to that vineyard is a planked gate,[185]
    That makes his opening with this bigger key:
    This other doth command a little door
    Which from the vineyard to the garden leads;
    There have I made my promise to call on him
    Upon the heavy middle of the night.
DUKE. But shall you on your knowledge find this way?
ISABELLA. I have ta'en a due and wary note upon't;
    With whispering and most guilty diligence,
    In action all of precept,[186] he did show me
    The way twice o'er.
DUKE. Are there no other tokens
    Between you 'greed concerning her observance?
ISABELLA. No, none, but only a repair i' the dark;
    And that I have possess'd him[187] my most stay
    Can be but brief: for I have made him know
    I have a servant comes with me along,
    That stays upon me; whose persuasion is
    I come about my brother.
DUKE. 'Tis well borne up.

---

[183] *Meet* is used rather strangely here, and perhaps there is some fault in the text. But we find a like instance in *Cymbeline*, i. 1: "When shall we *see* again?"

[184] *Circummured* is, literally, *walled around*. The word does not occur again in Shakespeare.

[185] "A planched gate" is simply a gate *made of planks*.—In the next line, *his* refers to *gate*; the old substitute for *its*, which was not then an accepted word.

[186] "Action *all of precept*" is, I take it, action *altogether preceptive*, or giving directions wholly by action. In like manner, the Poet repeatedly has "be *of comfort*" for *be comforted*. And *all* for *altogether* is used very often by Spenser, and several times by Shakespeare.

[187] The use of to *possess* for to *inform*, or to *assure*, is quite frequent.

I have not yet made known to Mariana
A word of this.—What ho, within! come forth.

[*Re-enter* MARIANA.]

I pray you be acquainted with this maid;
She comes to do you good.
ISABELLA. I do desire the like.
DUKE. Do you persuade yourself that I respect you?
MARIANA. Good friar, I know you do, and have found it.
DUKE. Take, then, this your companion by the hand,
Who hath a story ready for your ear:
I shall attend your leisure:[188] but make haste;
The vaporous night approaches.
MARIANA. Will't please you walk aside?

[*Exeunt* MARIANA *and* ISABELLA.]

DUKE. O place and greatness, millions of false eyes
Are stuck upon thee! volumes of report
Run with these false, and most contrarious quests[189]
Upon thy doings! thousand 'scapes of wit[190]
Make thee the father of their idle dream,
And rack thee in their fancies!—

[*Re-enter* MARIANA *and* ISABELLA.]

Welcome! how agreed?
ISABELLA. She'll take the enterprise upon her, father,
If you advise it.
DUKE. 'Tis not my consent,
But my entreaty too.
ISABELLA. Little have you to say,
When you depart from him, but, soft and low,
Remember now my brother.
MARIANA. Fear me not.
DUKE. Nor, gentle daughter, fear you not at all;
He is your husband on a pre-contract:
To bring you thus together 'tis no sin,
Sith that the justice of your title to him

---

[188] "*Wait for* you *to be at* leisure." *Attend* is often thus equivalent to *wait for.*

[189] *Quests*, here, is *inquiries, questionings*, or *inquisitions*.

[190] *'Scapes of wit* are *sportive sallies* or *flights*. The Poet has, I think, no other instance of *escape* or *'scape* so used; though we have, in *King John*, iii. 4, "No *'scape* of Nature"; where *'scape* means *freak*, or *irregularity*.

Doth flourish[191] the deceit. Come, let us go;
Our corn's to reap, for yet our tithe's to sow.[192] [*Exeunt.*]

SCENE II.

A Room in the Prison.

[*Enter the* PROVOST *and* POMPEY.]

PROVOST. Come hither, sirrah. Can you cut off a man's head?

POMPEY. If the man be a bachelor, sir, I can: but if he be a married
man, he's his wife's head, and I can never cut off a woman's head.

PROVOST. Come, sir, leave me your snatches and yield me a direct
answer. To-morrow morning are to die Claudio and Barnardine.
Here is in our prison a common executioner, who in his office
lacks a helper; if you will take it on you to assist him, it shall
redeem you from your gyves; if not, you shall have your full time
of imprisonment, and your deliverance with an unpitied[193]
whipping; for you have been a notorious bawd.

POMPEY. Sir, I have been an unlawful bawd time out of mind; but yet
I will be content to be a lawful hangman. I would be glad to
receive some instruction from my fellow-partner.

PROVOST. What ho, Abhorson! Where's Abhorson, there?

[*Enter* ABHORSON.]

ABHORSON. Do you call, sir?

PROVOST. Sirrah, here's a fellow will help you to-morrow in your
execution. If you think it meet, compound with him by the year,
and let him abide here with you; if not, use him for the present, and
dismiss him. He cannot plead his estimation with you; he hath been
a bawd.

ABHORSON. A bawd, sir? Fie upon him; he will discredit our
mystery.

PROVOST. Go to, sir; you weigh equally; a feather will turn the scale.
[*Exit.*]

POMPEY. Pray, sir, by your good favour,—for, surely, sir, a good
favour you have, but that you have a hanging look,—do you call,
sir, your occupation a mystery?

ABHORSON. Ay, sir; a mystery.

POMPEY. Painting, sir, I have heard say, is a mystery; and your

---

[191] To *flourish* a thing, as the word is here used, is to *make it fair*, or to take the
ugliness out of it.

[192] *Tilth* here means land made ready for sowing.

[193] *Unpitied* for *pitiless* or *unpitiable*; that is, *merciless.* See page 64, note 156.

whores, sir, being members of my occupation, using painting, do prove my occupation a mystery: but what mystery there should be in hanging, if I should be hanged, I cannot imagine.

ABHORSON. Sir, it is a mystery.

POMPEY. Proof.

ABHORSON. Every true man's[194] apparel fits your thief: if it be too little for your thief, your true man thinks it big enough; if it be too big for your thief, your thief thinks it little enough; so every true man's apparel fits your thief.

[*Re-enter the* PROVOST.]

PROVOST. Are you agreed?

POMPEY. Sir, I will serve him; for I do find your hangman is a more penitent trade than your bawd; he doth oftener ask forgiveness.[195]

PROVOST. You, sirrah, provide your block and your axe to-morrow four o'clock.

ABHORSON. Come on, bawd; I will instruct thee in my trade; follow.

POMPEY. I do desire to learn, sir; and I hope, if you have occasion to use me for your own turn, you shall find me yare;[196] for truly, sir, for your kindness I owe you a good turn.

PROVOST. Call hither Barnardine and Claudio.

[*Exeunt* POMPEY *and* ABHORSON.]

One has my pity; not a jot the other,
Being a murderer, though he were my brother.—

[*Enter* CLAUDIO.]

Look, here's the warrant, Claudio, for thy death:
'Tis now dead midnight, and by eight to-morrow
Thou must be made immortal. Where's Barnardine?

CLAUDIO. As fast lock'd up in sleep as guiltless labour

---

[194] A *true* man is, in old language, an *honest* man; and so the opposite of a *thief.*— *Mystery* was much used formerly, as it still is sometimes, for *at t* or *trade.*—The cogency, or the relevancy, of Abhorson's proof is not very apparent. Heath's explanation is probably right; in substance as follows: Abhorson adopts the same method of argument which Pompey has used a little before; and, as Pompey enrolls the fast girls of his fraternity under the art of painting, so Abhorson "lays claim to the thieves as members of his occupation, and in their right endeavours to rank his brethren, the hangmen, under the mystery of fitters of apparel or tailors."

[195] The executioner, just before doing his office, used always to ask forgiveness of the person in hand.

[196] *Yare* is *nimble* or *spry.*

When it lies starkly[197] in the traveller's bones:
He will not wake.
PROVOST. Who can do good on him?
Well, go, prepare yourself. [*Knocking within.*] But hark, what
noise?
Heaven give your spirits comfort!

[*Exit* CLAUDIO.]

—By and by!—
I hope it is some pardon or reprieve
For the most gentle Claudio.—Welcome, father.

[*Enter the* DUKE *disguised as before.*]

DUKE. The best and wholesomest spirits of the night
Envelop you, good Provost! Who call'd here of late?
PROVOST. None, since the curfew rung.
DUKE. Not Isabel?
PROVOST. No.
DUKE. They will then, ere't be long.
PROVOST. What comfort is for Claudio?
DUKE. There's some in hope.
PROVOST. It is a bitter deputy.
DUKE. Not so, not so: his life is parallel'd
Even with the stroke[198] and line of his great justice;
He doth with holy abstinence subdue
That in himself which he spurs on his power
To qualify[199] in others: were he meal'd[200] with that
Which he corrects, then were he tyrannous;
But this being so, he's just. [*Knocking within.*]
Now are they come.—

[*Exit* PROVOST.]

This is a gentle Provost: seldom-when[201]
The steeled gaoler is the friend of men.—
How now? what noise? That spirit's possess'd with haste
That wounds th' unlisting[202] postern with these strokes.

---

[197] *Stiffly*; *stiff* being one of the old meanings of *stark*.

[198] The stroke of a pen; that is, *mark*; hence, perhaps, *rule*.

[199] *Qualify* here means *temper, moderate, reduce*.

[200] *Meal'd* is, probably, *mingled, compounded*, or *made up*; from the French *mesler*.
Some, however, explain it *over-dusted* or *defiled*.

[201] *Seldom-when* is simply *seldom*; used here for the sake of the rhyme.

[*Re-enter the* PROVOST.]

PROVOST. [*Speaking to one at the door.*] There he must stay until the
    officer
Arise to let him in; he is call'd up.
DUKE. Have you no countermand for Claudio yet,
    But he must die to-morrow?
PROVOST. None, sir, none.
DUKE. As near the dawning, Provost, as it is,
    You shall hear more ere morning.
PROVOST. Happily[203]
    You something know; yet I believe there comes
    No countermand; no such example have we:
    Besides, upon the very siege[204] of justice,
    Lord Angelo hath to the public ear
    Profess'd the contrary.

[*Enter a* MESSENGER.]

    This is his lordship's man.
DUKE. And here comes Claudio's pardon.
MESSENGER. [*Giving a paper.*] My lord hath sent you this note; and
    by me this further charge, that you swerve not from the smallest
    article of it, neither in time, matter, or other circumstance. Good
    morrow; for as I take it, it is almost day.
PROVOST. I shall obey him.

[*Exit* MESSENGER.]

DUKE. [*Aside.*] This is his pardon, purchased by such sin,
    For which the pardoner himself is in:
    Hence hath offence his[205] quick celerity,
    When it is borne in high authority:
    When vice makes mercy, mercy's so extended
    That for the fault's love is the offender friended.—
    Now, sir, what news?

---

[202] *Unsisting*, as Blackstone says, "may signify *never at rest.*"
[203] *Happily* for *haply*, or *perhaps*. The Poet often makes it a trisyllable, to fill up his
verse.
[204] *Siege* was in common use for *seat*. So in *The Faerie Queene*, ii. 4, 44:

    A stately *siege* of soveraine majestye,
    And thereon satt a Woman gorgeous gay.

[205] *His* for *its* again. See page 71, note 185.

PROVOST. I told you: Lord Angelo, belike thinking me remiss in mine office, awakens me with this unwonted putting-on;[206] methinks strangely, for he hath not used it before.

DUKE. Pray you, let's hear.

PROVOST. [*Reads.*] *Whatsoever you may hear to the contrary, let Claudio be executed by four of the clock; and, in the afternoon, Barnardine: for my better satisfaction, let me have Claudio's head sent me by five. Let this be duly performed; with a thought that more depends on it than we must yet deliver. Thus fail not to do your office, as you will answer it at your peril.—*

What say you to this, sir?

DUKE. What is that Barnardine who is to be executed in the afternoon?

PROVOST. A Bohemian born; but here nursed up and bred: one that is a prisoner nine years old.[207]

DUKE. How came it that the absent Duke had not either delivered him to his liberty or executed him? I have heard it was ever his manner to do so.

PROVOST. His friends still wrought reprieves for him; and, indeed, his fact,[208] till now in the government of Lord Angelo, came not to an undoubtful proof.

DUKE. It is now apparent?

PROVOST. Most manifest, and not denied by himself.

DUKE. Hath he borne himself penitently in prison? How seems he to be touched?

PROVOST. A man that apprehends death no more dreadfully but as a drunken sleep; careless, reckless, and fearless, of what's past, present, or to come; insensible of mortality and desperately mortal.

DUKE. He wants advice.

PROVOST. He will hear none; he hath evermore had the liberty of the prison; give him leave to escape hence, he would not: drunk many times a-day, if not many days entirely drunk. We have very oft awaked him, as if to carry him to execution, and showed him a seeming warrant for it: it hath not moved him at all.

DUKE. More of him anon. There is written in your brow, Provost, honesty and constancy: if I read it not truly, my ancient skill beguiles me; but in the boldness of my cunning,[209] I will lay myself in hazard. Claudio, whom here you have warrant to execute, is no

---

[206] *Putting-on* is *prompting, instigation,* or *setting on.* Often so.

[207] One that had been in prison nine years.

[208] *Fact,* like the Latin *factum,* is, properly, *deed;* but here means *crime.* So in the next Act: "Should she kneel down in mercy of this *fact,* her brother's ghost his paved bed would break," &c.

[209] "In the *confidence* of my *sagacity*" is the meaning. So both *boldness* and *cunning* were not unfrequently used.

greater forfeit to the law than Angelo who hath sentenced him. To make you understand this in a manifested effect, I crave but four days' respite; for the which you are to do me both a present and a dangerous courtesy.

PROVOST. Pray, sir, in what?

DUKE. In the delaying death.

PROVOST. Alack, how may I do it? having the hour limited,[210] and an express command, under penalty, to deliver his head in the view of Angelo? I may make my case as Claudio's, to cross this in the smallest.

DUKE. By the vow of mine order, I warrant you, if my instructions may be your guide. Let this Barnardine be this morning executed, and his head borne to Angelo.

PROVOST. Angelo hath seen them both, and will discover the favour.

DUKE. O, death's a great disguiser: and you may add to it. Shave the head and tie the beard; and say it was the desire of the penitent to be so bared before his death. You know the course is common. If anything fall to you upon this, more than thanks and good fortune, by the saint whom I profess, I will plead against it with my life.

PROVOST. Pardon me, good father; it is against my oath.

DUKE. Were you sworn to the Duke, or to the deputy?

PROVOST. To him and to his substitutes.

DUKE. You will think you have made no offence if the Duke avouch the justice of your dealing?

PROVOST. But what likelihood is in that?

DUKE. Not a resemblance, but a certainty. Yet since I see you fearful, that neither my coat, integrity, nor persuasion, can with ease attempt you, I will go further than I meant, to pluck all fears out of you. Look you, sir, here is the hand and seal of the Duke. You know the character, I doubt not; and the signet is not strange to you.

PROVOST. I know them both.

DUKE. The contents of this is the return of the Duke; you shall anon over-read it at your pleasure, where you shall find within these two days he will be here. This is a thing that Angelo knows not: for he this very day receives letters of strange tenour: perchance of the Duke's death; perchance entering into some monastery; but, by chance, nothing of what is writ. Look, the unfolding star calls up the shepherd.[211] Put not yourself into amazement how these things should be: all difficulties are but easy when they are known. Call

---

[210] *Limited*, here, is *appointed*. The Poet repeatedly uses it thus. So, before, in iii. 1: "between which time of the contract and *limit* of the solemnity;" where *limit* means *appointed time*.

[211] The star that bids the shepherd fold
Now the top of heaven doth hold.—COMUS.

your executioner, and off with Barnardine's head: I will give him a present shrift,[212] and advise him for a better place. Yet you are amazed: but this shall absolutely resolve[213] you. Come away; it is almost clear dawn. [*Exeunt.*]

SCENE III.

Another Room in the Same.

[*Enter* POMPEY.]

POMPEY. I am as well acquainted here as I was in our house of profession: one would think it were Mistress Overdone's own house, for here be many of her old customers. First, here's young Master Rash;[214] he's in for a commodity of brown paper and old ginger,[215] nine score and seventeen pounds; of which he made five marks ready money: marry, then ginger was not much in request, for the old women were all dead. Then is there here one Master Caper, at the suit of Master Three-pile the mercer, for some four suits of peach-coloured satin, which now peaches[216] him a beggar. Then have we here young Dizzy, and young Master Deepvow, and Master Copperspur, and Master Starve-lackey, the rapier and dagger man, and young Drop-hair that killed lusty Pudding, and Master Forthright the tilter, and brave Master Shoe-tie the great traveller, and wild Half-can that stabbed Pots, and, I think, forty more; all great doers in our trade, and are now *for the Lord's sake*.[217]

---

[212] *Shrift* is the old word for *confession* and *absolution.*

[213] *Resolve* is *assure* or *satisfy.* See page 60, note 148.

[214] This and the following names are all meant to be characteristic. *Rash* was a silken fabric formerly worn in coats.

[215] Lenders of money were wont to advance part of a given sum in cash, and the rest in goods of little value, such as they could hardly get rid of otherwise. It appears that *brown paper* and *ginger* were often among the articles so put off upon borrowers. So in *Greene's Defence of Coney-catching*, 1592: "If he borrow a hundred pound, he shall have forty in silver, and threescore in wares; as lute-strings, hobby-horses, or *brown paper!*' Also in Greene's *Quip for an Upstart Courtier*: "For the merchant delivered the iron, tin, lead, hops, sugars, spices, oils, *brown paper*, or whatsoever else, from six months to six months; which when the poor gentleman came to sell again, he could not make threescore and ten in the hundred besides the usury." Staunton notes upon the matter thus: "The practice, no doubt, originated in a desire to evade the penalties for usury, and must have reached an alarming height, as the old writers make it a perpetual mark for satire."

[216] To *peach* is to *accuse, inform against,* or *impeach.* So, when Falstaff says, "I'll *peach* for this," he means "I'll turn State's evidence"; that is, testify against his accomplices.

[217] This appears to have been the language in which prisoners confined for debt addressed passers-by. So in Nash's *Pierce Penniless*, 1593: "At that time that thy joys were in the *fleeting*, and thus crying *for the Lord's sake* out of an iron window." And in

[*Enter* ABHORSON.]

ABHORSON. Sirrah, bring Barnardine hither.
POMPEY. Master Barnardine! You must rise and be hanged, Master
    Barnardine!
ABHORSON. What ho, Barnardine!
BARNARDINE. [*Within.*] A pox o' your throats! Who makes that
    noise there? What are you?
POMPEY. Your friend, sir; the hangman. You must be so good, sir, to
    rise and be put to death.
BARNARDINE. [*Within.*] Away, you rogue, away; I am sleepy.
ABHORSON. Tell him he must awake, and that quickly too.
POMPEY. Pray, Master Barnardine, awake till you are executed, and
    sleep afterwards.
ABHORSON. Go in to him, and fetch him out.
POMPEY. He is coming, sir, he is coming; I hear his straw rustle.

[*Enter* BARNARDINE.]

ABHORSON. Is the axe upon the block, sirrah?
POMPEY. Very ready, sir.
BARNARDINE. How now, Abhorson? what's the news with you?
ABHORSON. Truly, sir, I would desire you to clap into your prayers;
    for, look you, the warrant's come.
BARNARDINE. You rogue, I have been drinking all night; I am not
    fitted for't.
POMPEY. O, the better, sir; for he that drinks all night and is hanged
    betimes in the morning may sleep the sounder all the next day.

[*Enter the* DUKE *disguised as before.*]

ABHORSON. Look you, sir, here comes your ghostly father. Do we
    jest now, think you?
DUKE. Sir, induced by my charity, and hearing how hastily you are to
    depart, I am come to advise you, comfort you, and pray with you.
BARNARDINE. Friar, not I; I have been drinking hard all night, and I
    will have more time to prepare me, or they shall beat out my brains
    with billets: I will not consent to die this day, that's certain.
DUKE. O, Sir, you must; and therefore I beseech you,
    Look forward on the journey you shall go.

Davies' *Epigrams*, 1611: "Good gentle writers, *for the Lord's sake, for the Lord's sake*,
like *Ludgate prisoners*, lo, I, begging, make my mone."—*Fleeting* refers to the *Fleet
prison.*

BARNARDINE. I swear I will not die to-day for any man's persuasion.
DUKE. But hear you,—
BARNARDINE. Not a word; if you have anything to say to me, come
    to my ward; for thence will not I to-day. [*Exit.*]
DUKE. Unfit to live or die. O gravel heart!—
    After him, fellows; bring him to the block.

    [*Exeunt* ABHORSON *and* POMPEY.]

    [*Re-enter the* PROVOST.]

PROVOST. Now, sir, how do you find the prisoner?
DUKE.A creature unprepar'd, unmeet for death;
    And to transport him in the mind he is
    Were damnable.
PROVOST. Here in the prison, father,
    There died this morning of a cruel fever
    One Ragozine, a most notorious pirate,
    A man of Claudio's years; his beard and head
    Just of his colour. What if we do omit
    This reprobate till he were well inclined;
    And satisfy the deputy with the visage
    Of Ragozine, more like to Claudio?
DUKE. O, 'tis an accident that Heaven provides!
    Despatch it presently; the hour draws on
    Prefix'd by Angelo: see this be done,
    And sent according to command; whiles I
    Persuade this rude wretch willingly to die.
PROVOST. This shall be done, good father, presently.
    But Barnardine must die this afternoon:
    And how shall we continue Claudio,
    To save me from the danger that might come
    If he were known alive?
DUKE. Let this be done,—put them in secret holds,
    Both Barnardine and Claudio:
    Ere twice the sun hath made his journal greeting
    To th' under generation,[218] you shall find
    Your safety manifested.
PROVOST. I am your free dependant.
DUKE. Quick, dispatch, and send the head to Angelo.—

---

[218] "Th' *under* generation "means the generation living on the earth beneath; those
inhabiting what the Poet describes in *King Lear* as "this *under* globe," and in *The
Tempest* as "this *lower* world."—*Journal* is used in its proper literal sense, *daily*.

[*Exit* PROVOST.]

Now will I write letters to Angelo,—
The Provost, he shall bear them,—whose contents
Shall witness to him I am near at home,
And that, by great injunctions, I am bound
To enter publicly: him I'll desire
To meet me at the consecrated fount,
A league below the city; and from thence,
By cold gradation and well-balanced form.
We shall proceed with Angelo.

[*Re-enter the* PROVOST *with* RAGOZINE's *head.*]

PROVOST. Here is the head; I'll carry it myself.
DUKE. Convenient is it. Make a swift return;
    For I would commune with you of such things
    That want no ear but yours.
PROVOST. I'll make all speed. [*Exit.*]
ISABELLA. [*Within.*] Peace, ho, be here!
DUKE. The tongue of Isabel.—She's come to know
    If yet her brother's pardon be come hither:
    But I will keep her ignorant of her good,
    To make her heavenly comforts of despair
    When it is least expected.

[*Enter* ISABELLA.]

ISABELLA. Ho, by your leave!
DUKE. Good morning to you, fair and gracious daughter.
ISABELLA. The better, given me by so holy a man.
    Hath yet the deputy sent my brother's pardon?
DUKE. He hath released him, Isabel, from the world:
    His head is off and sent to Angelo.
ISABELLA. Nay, but it is not so.
DUKE. It is no other:
    Show your wisdom, daughter, in your close patience.
ISABELLA. O, I will to him and pluck out his eyes!
DUKE. You shall[219] not be admitted to his sight.
ISABELLA. [*Weeping.*] Unhappy Claudio! Wretched Isabel!
    Injurious world! Most damned Angelo!
DUKE. This nor hurts him nor profits you a jot:

---

[219] *Shall* for *will*, in accordance with the usage of the time. So, a little after, "you *shall* find"; and several times before in this scene.

Forbear it, therefore; give your cause to Heaven.
Mark what I say; which you shall find
By every syllable a faithful verity:
The Duke comes home to-morrow;—nay, dry your eyes:—
One of our convent, and his confessor,
Gives me this instance:[220] Already he hath carried
Notice to Escalus and Angelo,
Who do prepare to meet him at the gates,
There to give up their power. If you can, pace your wisdom
In that good path that I would wish it go,
And you shall have your bosom[221] on this wretch,
Grace of the Duke, revenges to your heart,
And general Honour.
ISABELLA. I am directed by you.
DUKE. This letter, then, to Friar Peter give;
'Tis that he sent me of the Duke's return.
Say, by this token, I desire his company
At Mariana's house to-night. Her cause and yours
I'll perfect him withal; and he shall bring you
Before the Duke; and to the head of Angelo
Accuse him home, and home.[222] For my poor self,
I am combined[223] by a sacred vow,
And shall be absent. Wend you with this letter:
Command these fretting waters from your eyes
With a light heart; trust not my holy order,
If I pervert your course.—Who's here?

[*Enter* LUCIO.]

LUCIO. Good even. Friar, where is the Provost?
DUKE. Not within, sir.
LUCIO. O pretty Isabella, I am pale at mine heart to see thine eyes so red; thou must be patient: I am fain to dine and sup with water and bran; I dare not for my head fill my belly; one fruitful meal would set me to't. But they say the Duke will be here to-morrow. By my troth, Isabel, I loved thy brother. If the old fantastical Duke of dark corners had been at home, he had lived.

[*Exit* ISABELLA.]

---

[220] *Instance* is *assurance*, or *circumstance in proof.*

[221] *Bosom* for *wish* or *desire*, of which it is the seat.

[222] *Home* is much used by the Poet for *thoroughly, to the uttermost,* or *to the quick.* The repetition here gives a very strong sense.

[223] *Bound* or *pledged*; like *combinate* before. See page 61, note 149.

DUKE. Sir, the Duke is marvellous little beholding to your reports; but the best is, he lives not in them.

LUCIO. Friar, thou knowest not the Duke so well as I do: he's a better woodman[224] than thou takest him for.

DUKE. Well, you'll answer this one day. Fare ye well.

LUCIO. Nay, tarry; I'll go along with thee; I can tell thee pretty tales of the Duke.

DUKE. You have told me too many of him already, sir, if they be true: if not true, none were enough.

LUCIO. I was once before him for getting a wench with child.

DUKE. Did you such a thing?

LUCIO. Yes, marry, did I; but I was fain to forswear it: they would else have married me to the rotten medlar.

DUKE. Sir, your company is fairer than honest. Rest you well.

LUCIO. By my troth, I'll go with thee to the lane's end. If bawdy talk offend you, we'll have very little of it. Nay, friar, I am a kind of burr; I shall stick. [*Exeunt.*]

SCENE IV.

A Room in ANGELO'*s House.*

[*Enter* ANGELO *and* ESCALUS.]

ESCALUS. Every letter he hath writ hath disvouched other.

ANGELO. In most uneven and distracted manner. His actions show much like to madness; pray Heaven his wisdom be not tainted! And why meet him at the gates, and re-deliver our authorities there?

ESCALUS. I guess not.

ANGELO. And why should we proclaim it in an hour before his entering that, if any crave redress of injustice, they should exhibit their petitions in the street?

ESCALUS. He shows his reason for that;—to have a dispatch of complaints; and to deliver us from devices hereafter, which shall then have no power to stand against us.

ANGELO. Well, I beseech you, let it be proclaim'd:
Betimes i' the morn I'll call you at your house:
Give notice to such men of sort and suit[225]

---

[224] A *woodman* is a *hunter*; here the word is used for one who hunts female game; the usage having perhaps sprung from the consonance of *dear* and *deer*.

[225] *Sort*, here, is *rank*; a sense in which Shakespeare uses the word repeatedly.—In the feudal times all vassals were bound to be always ready to attend and serve their superior lord, when summoned either to his courts or to his standard. This was called suit-service; and such appears to be the intention of *suit* in the text.

As are to meet him.
ESCALUS. I shall, sir: fare you well.
ANGELO. Good night.—

[*Exit* ESCALUS.]

This deed unshapes me quite, makes me unpregnant,[226]
And dull to all proceedings. A deflower'd maid!
And by an eminent body that enforced
The law against it!—But that her tender shame
Will not proclaim against her maiden loss,
How might she tongue me? Yet reason dares her no;[227]
For my authority bears a so credent bulk,[228]
That no particular scandal once can touch
But it confounds the breather. He should have liv'd,
Save that his riotous youth, with dangerous sense,
Might in the times to come have ta'en revenge,
By so receiving a dishonour'd life
With ransom of such shame. Would yet he had liv'd!
Alack, when once our grace we have forgot,
Nothing goes right,—we would, and we would not. [*Exit.*]

SCENE V.

Fields without the Town.

[*Enter the* DUKE *in his own habit, and Friar* PETER.]

DUKE. These letters at fit time deliver me. [*Giving letters.*]
The Provost knows our purpose and our plot.
The matter being afoot, keep your instruction
And hold you ever to our special drift;
Though sometimes you do blench[229] from this to that
As cause doth minister. Go, call at Flavius' house,

---

[226] *Unpregnant* here is the opposite of *pregnant* as explained, page 18, note 4; *unprepared* or *at a loss.*

[227] Reason *warns* or *challenges* her not to do it, cries *no* to her whenever she is moved to do it. The phrase is somewhat strange; but the Poet elsewhere uses *dare* in a similar way, and a like use of *no* is not uncommon. So Beaumont and Fletcher, in *The Chances*, iii. 4: "I wear a sword to satisfy the world *no*;" that is, to satisfy the world *'tis not so.* And in *A Wife for a Month*: "I'm sure he did not, for I charg'd him *no*;" that is, plainly, charged him *not to do it.*

[228] My authority carries such a *strength of credibility*, or a force so great for inspiring belief or confidence. A very peculiar use of *credent.—Particular*, in the next line, means *private.*

[229] To *blench* is to *start* or *fly off.*

And tell him where I stay: give the like notice
To Valentinus, Rowland, and to Crassus,
And bid them bring the trumpets to the gate;
But send me Flavius first.
PETER. It shall be speeded well. [*Exit.*]

[*Enter* VARRIUS.]

DUKE. I thank thee, Varrius; thou hast made good haste:
Come, we will walk. There's other of our friends
Will greet us here anon, my gentle Varrius. [*Exeunt.*]

SCENE VI.

Street near the City-gate.

[*Enter* ISABELLA *and* MARIANA.]

ISABELLA. To speak so indirectly[230] I am loath;
I would say the truth; but to accuse him so,
That is your part: yet I am advis'd to do it;
He says, to 'vailfull purpose.
MARIANA. Be ruled by him.
ISABELLA. Besides, he tells me that, if peradventure
He speak against me on the adverse side,
I should not think it strange; for 'tis a physic
That's bitter to sweet end.
MARIANA. I would Friar Peter.—
ISABELLA. O, peace! the friar is come.

[*Enter Friar* PETER.]

PETER. Come, I have found you out a stand most fit,
Where you may have such vantage on the Duke
He shall not pass you. Twice have the trumpets sounded;
The generous and gravest[231] citizens
Have hent[232] the gates, and very near upon

---

[230] To speak *indirectly* here means to speak *falsely* or *untruly*. *Indirection* bears the same sense in *Hamlet*, ii. 1: "And thus do we by indirections find directions out."

[231] The force of the superlative in *gravest* here is meant to retroact on *generous*, which is used withal in its Latin sense, *well-born*: *noblest* and *gravest*. The Poet has many instances of like construction. So in *The Merchant*, iii. 2: "The best condition'd and unwearied spirit." Here the superlative in *best* is continued over *unwearied* in the sense of *most*.

[232] To *hent* is to *seize* or *take possession of*.

The Duke is entering; therefore, hence, away. [*Exeunt.*]

ACT V.

SCENE I.

A public Place near the City-gate.

[MARIANA *veiled*, ISABELLA, *and Friar* PETER, *behind. Enter, from one side, the* DUKE *in his own habit*, VARRIUS, LORDS; *from the other*, ANGELO, ESCALUS, LUCIO, *the* PROVOST, OFFICERS, *and* CITIZENS.]

DUKE. My very worthy cousin, fairly met:—
    Our old and faithful friend, we are glad to see you.
ANGELO and ESCALUS. Happy return be to your royal grace!
DUKE. Many and hearty thankings to you both.
    We have made inquiry of you; and we hear
    Such goodness of your justice that our soul
    Cannot but yield you forth to public thanks,
    Forerunning more requital.
ANGELO. You make my bonds[233] still greater.
DUKE. O, your desert speaks loud; and I should wrong it
    To lock it in the wards of covert bosom,
    When it deserves, with characters of brass,
    A forted residence 'gainst the tooth of time
    And rasure of oblivion. Give me your hand,
    And let the subject see, to make them know
    That outward courtesies would fain proclaim
    Favours that keep within.—Come, Escalus;
    You must walk by us on our other hand:—
    And good supporters are you.

[*Enter* PETER *and* ISABELLA *come forward.*]

PETER. Now is your time; speak loud, and kneel before him.
ISABELLA. Justice, O royal Duke! Vail[234] your regard
    Upon a wrong'd, I'd fain have said, a maid!
    O worthy prince, dishonour not your eye
    By throwing it on any other object
    Till you have heard me in my true complaint,
    And given me justice, justice, justice, justice!

---

[233] *Bonds* in the sense of *obligations.* Shakespeare repeatedly uses it thus.
[234] *Vail* is *cast down* or *let fall.* A common use of the word in the Poet's time.

DUKE. Relate your wrongs. In what? By whom? Be brief:
    Here is Lord Angelo shall give you justice.
    Reveal yourself to him.
ISABELLA. O worthy Duke,
    You bid me seek redemption of the devil:
    Hear me yourself; for that which I must speak
    Must either punish me, not being believ'd,
    Or wring redress from you; hear me, O, hear me here!
ANGELO. My lord, her wits, I fear me, are not firm:
    She hath been a suitor to me for her brother,
    Cut off by course of justice,—
ISABELLA. By course of justice!
ANGELO.—And she will speak most bitterly and strange.
ISABELLA. Most strange, but yet most truly, will I speak:
    That Angelo's forsworn, is it not strange?
    That Angelo's a murderer, is't not strange?
    That Angelo is an adulterous thief,
    An hypocrite, a virgin-violator,
    Is it not strange and strange?
DUKE. Nay, it is ten times strange.
ISABELLA. It is not truer he is Angelo
    Than this is all as true as it is strange:
    Nay, it is ten times true; for truth is truth
    To the end of reckoning.
DUKE. Away with her!—Poor soul,
    She speaks this in the infirmity of sense.
ISABELLA. O prince! I conjure[235] thee, as thou believ'st
    There is another comfort than this world,
    That thou neglect me not with that opinion
    That I am touch'd with madness: make not impossible
    That which but seems unlike; 'tis not impossible
    But one, the wicked'st caitiff on the ground,
    May seem as shy, as grave, as just, as absolute,
    As Angelo; even so may Angelo,
    In all his dressings, characts,[236] titles, forms,
    Be an arch-villain; believe it, royal prince,
    If he be less, he's nothing; but he's more,
    Had I more name for badness.
DUKE. By mine honesty,
    If she be mad,—as I believe no other,—
    Her madness hath the oddest frame of sense,

---

[235] *Conjure* had the accent indifferently on the first or second syllable, whether used in the sense of *earnestly entreat* or of practising magic.

[236] *Characts* is merely a shortened form of *characters*; here meaning *badges* or *marks of honour*.

Such a dependency of thing on thing,
As e'er I heard in madness.
ISABELLA. O gracious Duke,
    Harp not on that: nor do not banish reason
    For inequality;[237] but let your reason serve
    To make the truth appear where it seems hid
    And hide the false seems true.[238]
DUKE. Many that are not mad
    Have, sure, more lack of reason.—What would you say?
ISABELLA. I am the sister of one Claudio,
    Condemn'd upon the act of fornication
    To lose his head; condemn'd by Angelo:
    I, in probation of a sisterhood,
    Was sent to by my brother: one Lucio
    As then the messenger;—
LUCIO. That's I, an't like[239] your grace:
    I came to her from Claudio, and desir'd her
    To try her gracious fortune with Lord Angelo
    For her poor brother's pardon.
ISABELLA. That's he, indeed.
DUKE. You were not bid to speak.
LUCIO. No, my good lord;
    Nor wish'd to hold my peace.
DUKE. I wish you now, then;
    Pray you take note of it: and when you have
    A business for yourself, pray Heaven you then
    Be perfect.
LUCIO. I warrant your Honour.
DUKE. The warrant's for yourself; take heed to it.
ISABELLA. This gentleman told somewhat of my tale.
LUCIO. Right.
DUKE. It may be right; but you are in the wrong
    To speak before your time.—Proceed.
ISABELLA. I went
    To this pernicious caitiff deputy,—
DUKE. That's somewhat madly spoken.
ISABELLA. Pardon it;
    The phrase is to the matter.
DUKE. Mended again. The matter;—proceed.
ISABELLA. In brief,—to set the needless process by,

---

[237] Here *for* has the force of *because* or *on account* of. See page 33, note 58.— *Inequality* refers, I think, to the *different rank*, or *condition*, of the persons concerned; though it is commonly explained otherwise,—*apparent inconsistency* of speech.

[238] That is, the *falsehood which* seems true.

[239] *Like* for *please*; a frequent usage.

How I persuaded, how I pray'd, and kneel'd,
How he refell'd me, and how I replied,—
For this was of much length,—the vile conclusion
I now begin with grief and shame to utter:
He would not, but by gift of my chaste body
To his concupiscible intemperate lust,
Release my brother; and, after much debatement,
My sisterly remorse confutes[240] mine Honour,
And I did yield to him. But the next morn betimes,
His purpose surfeiting, he sends a warrant
For my poor brother's head.

DUKE. This is most likely!

ISABELLA. O, that it were as like as it is true!

DUKE. By Heaven, fond[241] wretch, thou know'st not what thou speak'st,
Or else thou art suborn'd against his Honour
In hateful practice.[242] First, his integrity
Stands without blemish:—next, it imports no reason
That with such vehemency he should pursue
Faults proper to himself: if he had so offended,
He would have weigh'd thy brother by himself,
And not have cut him off. Some one hath set you on;
Confess the truth, and say by whose advice
Thou camest here to complain.

ISABELLA. And is this all?
Then, O you blessed ministers above,
Keep me in patience; and, with ripen'd time,
Unfold the evil which is here wrapt up
In countenance![243]—Heaven shield your grace from woe,
As I, thus wrong'd, hence unbelieved go!

DUKE. I know you'd fain be gone.—An officer!
To prison with her!—Shall we thus permit
A blasting and a scandalous breath to fall
On him so near us? This needs must be a practice.—
Who knew of your intent and coming hither?

ISABELLA. One that I would were here, Friar Lodowick.

DUKE. A ghostly father, belike.—Who knows that Lodowick?

LUCIO. My lord, I know him; 'tis a meddling friar.

---

[240] *Remorse* is *pity* or *compassion.* See page 42, note 83.—*Confutes* is overcomes.—*Concupiscible,* second line before, is an instance of the passive form with the active sense; *concupiscent.*

[241] *Fond* is *foolish* or *silly;* generally used so in the Poet's time.

[242] *Practice* here means *stratagem* or *conspiracy.* So again a little after: "This needs must be *practice.*"

[243] *Countenance* for *specious appearance, well-acted hypocrisy.*

I do not like the man: had he been lay, my lord,
For certain words he spake against your grace
In your retirement, I had swing'd him soundly.
DUKE. Words against me? This's a good friar, belike!
And to set on this wretched woman here
Against our substitute!—Let this friar be found.
LUCIO. But yesternight, my lord, she and that friar,
I saw them at the prison: a saucy friar,
A very scurvy fellow.
PETER. Bless'd be your royal grace!
I have stood by, my lord, and I have heard
Your royal ear abus'd. First, hath this woman
Most wrongfully accus'd your substitute;
Who is as free from touch or soil with her
As she from one ungot.
DUKE. We did believe no less.
Know you that Friar Lodowick that she speaks of?
PETER. I know him for a man divine and holy;
Not scurvy, nor a temporary meddler,[244]
As he's reported by this gentleman;
And, on my trust, a man that never yet
Did, as he vouches, misreport your grace.
LUCIO. My lord, most villainously; believe it.
PETER. Well, he in time may come to clear himself;
But at this instant he is sick, my lord,
Of a strange fever. Upon his mere request,—
Being come to knowledge that there was complaint
Intended 'gainst Lord Angelo,—came I hither
To speak, as from his mouth, what he doth know
Is true and false; and what he, with his oath
And all probation, will make up full clear,
Whensoever he's convented.[245] First, for this woman—
To justify this worthy nobleman,
So vulgarly[246] and personally accused,—
Her shall you hear disproved to her eyes,
Till she herself confess it.
DUKE. Good friar, let's hear it.—

[ISABELLA *is carried off, guarded; and* MARIANA *comes
forward.*]

---

[244] *Temporary meddler* probably means one prone to meddle with *temporal affairs*; as some monks were said to be, notwithstanding their solemn renunciation of the world.

[245] *Convented* is *summoned* or *called to account*; brought face to face with his accusers.

[246] *Vulgarly* here means *publicly*; a classical use of the word.

Do you not smile at this, Lord Angelo?—
O Heaven! the vanity of wretched fools!
Give us some seats.—Come, cousin Angelo;
In this I'll be impartial;[247] be you judge
Of your own cause.—Is this the witness, friar?
First let her show her face, and after speak.

MARIANA. Pardon, my lord; I will not show my face
Until my husband bid me.

DUKE. What! are you married?

MARIANA. No, my lord.

DUKE. Are you a maid?

MARIANA. No, my lord.

DUKE. A widow, then?

MARIANA. Neither, my lord.

DUKE. Why, you are nothing then:—neither maid, widow, nor wife?

LUCIO. My lord, she may be a punk; for many of them are neither maid, widow, nor wife.

DUKE. Silence that fellow: I would he had some cause to prattle for himself.

LUCIO. Well, my lord.

MARIANA. My lord, I do confess I ne'er was married,
And I confess, besides, I am no maid:
I have known my husband; yet my husband knows not
That ever he knew me.

LUCIO. He was drunk, then, my lord; it can be no better.

DUKE. For the benefit of silence, would thou wert so too!

LUCIO. Well, my lord.

DUKE. This is no witness for Lord Angelo.

MARIANA. Now I come to't, my lord:
She that accuses him of fornication,
In self-same manner doth accuse my husband;
And charges him, my lord, with such a time
When I'll depose I had him in mine arms,
With all the effect of love.

ANGELO. Charges she more than me?

MARIANA. Not that I know.

DUKE. No? you say your husband.

MARIANA. Why, just, my lord, and that is Angelo,
Who thinks he knows that he ne'er knew my body,
But knows he thinks that he knows Isabel's.

ANGELO. This is a strange abuse.[248]—Let's see thy face.

---

[247] *Impartial* in the etymological sense of *taking no part*; *neutral*.

MARIANA. My husband bids me; now I will unmask.—[*Unveiling.*]
    This is that face, thou cruel Angelo,
    Which once thou swor'st was worth the looking on:
    This is the hand which, with a vow'd contract,
    Was fast belock'd in thine; this is the body
    That took away the match from Isabel,
    And did supply thee at thy garden-house[249]
    In her imagin'd person.
DUKE. Know you this woman?
LUCIO. Carnally, she says.
DUKE. Sirrah, no more.
LUCIO. Enough, my lord.
ANGELO. My lord, I must confess I know this woman;
    And five years since there was some speech of marriage
    Betwixt myself and her; which was broke off,
    Partly for that her promis'd proportions[250]
    Came short of composition; but in chief
    For that her reputation was disvalued
    In levity: since which time of five years
    I never spake with her, saw her, nor heard from her,
    Upon my faith and Honour.
MARIANA. Noble prince,
    As there comes light from Heaven and words from breath,
    As there is sense in truth and truth in virtue,
    I am affianc'd this man's wife as strongly
    As words could make up vows: and, my good lord,
    But Tuesday night last gone, in his garden-house,
    He knew me as a wife. As this is true,
    Let me in safety raise me from my knees,
    Or else for ever be confixed here,
    A marble monument!
ANGELO. I did but smile till now;
    Now, good my lord, give me the scope of justice;
    My patience here is touch'd. I do perceive
    These poor informal[251] women are no more
    But instruments of some more mightier member
    That sets them on. Let me have way, my lord,

---

[248] *Abuse* for *deception* or *imposture*; the more common meaning of the word in Shakespeare's time.

[249] A *garden-house* is much the same as what we call a *summer-house.* Such houses were common in the suburban gardens of London, and were often used as places of intrigue and clandestine meeting.

[250] Probably meaning, her fortune which was promised to be proportionable to his own.—Composition is *agreement, contract.*

[251] *Informal* was used of *crazy* persons; that is, persons whose minds were *out of form.*

    To find this practice out.
DUKE. Ay, with my heart;
    And punish them to your height of pleasure.—
    Thou foolish friar, and thou pernicious woman,
    Compact with her that's gone, think'st thou thy oaths,
    Though they would swear down each particular saint,
    Were testimonies against his worth and credit,
    That's seal'd in approbation?[252]—You, Lord Escalus,
    Sit with my cousin; lend him your kind pains
    To find out this abuse, whence 'tis derived.—
    There is another friar that set them on;
    Let him be sent for.
PETER. Would lie were here, my lord; for he indeed
    Hath set the women on to this complaint:
    Your Provost knows the place where he abides,
    And he may fetch him.
DUKE. Go, do it instantly.—

    [*Exit* PROVOST.]

    And you, my noble and well-warranted cousin,
    Whom it concerns to hear this matter forth,[253]
    Do with your injuries as seems you best
    In any chastisement. I for a while
    Will leave you: but stir not you till you have well
    Determined upon these slanderers.
ESCALUS. My lord, we'll do it throughly.—

    [*Exit* DUKE.]

    Signior Lucio, did not you say you knew that Friar Lodowick to be
    a dishonest person?
LUCIO. *Cucullus non facit monachum:*[254] honest in nothing but in his
    clothes; and one that hath spoke most villainous speeches of the
    Duke.
ESCALUS. We shall entreat you to abide here till he come and enforce
    them against him: we shall find this friar a notable fellow.
LUCIO. As any in Vienna, on my word.

---

[252] *Seal'd in approbation* is the same in sense as having *a ratified approval* or *a certified attestation*; or as *being proved beyond question.* The sealing of a bond or contract is that which *finishes* it, or gives it full force and validity.

[253] "To hear this matter *out,*" or *to the end.* A frequent use of *forth.*

[254] "A cowl does not make a monk." A proverbial saying, used again in *Twelfth Night*, i. 5, where the application of it is, "wearing a Fool's dress does not make the wearer a fool."

ESCALUS. Call that same Isabel here once again; I would speak with
her.

[*Exit an* ATTENDANT.]

—Pray you, my lord, give me leave to question; you shall see how
I'll handle her.
LUCIO. Not better than he, by her own report.
ESCALUS. Say you?
LUCIO. Marry, sir, I think, if you handled her privately, she would
sooner confess: perchance, publicly, she'll be ashamed.
ESCALUS. I will go darkly to work with her.
LUCIO. That's the way; for women are light at midnight.[255]

[*Re-enter* OFFICERS *with* ISABELLA.]

ESCALUS. [*To* ISABELLA.] Come on, mistress; here's a
gentlewoman denies all that you have said.
LUCIO. My lord, here comes the rascal I spoke of, here with the
Provost.
ESCALUS. In very good time:—speak not you to him till we call upon
you.
LUCIO. Mum.

[*Re-enter the* DUKE *disguised as a Friar, and the* PROVOST.]

ESCALUS. Come, sir: did you set these women on to slander Lord
Angelo? they have confessed you did.
DUKE. 'Tis false.
ESCALUS. How! Know you where you are?
DUKE. Respect to your great place! and let the devil
Be sometime Honour'd for his burning throne![256]—
Where is the Duke? 'tis he should hear me speak.
ESCALUS. The Duke's in us; and we will hear you speak:
Look you speak justly.
DUKE. Boldly, at least.—But, O, poor souls,
Come you to seek the lamb here of the fox,
Good night to your redress! Is the Duke gone?
Then is your cause gone too. The Duke's unjust

---

[255] This is well explained in *The Merchant*, v. 1, where Portia says, "Let me give light, but let me not be light; for a *light wife doth make a heavy husband.*"

[256] I am not quite clear whether the meaning here is, that the Devil *should*, or that he *should not*, be sometimes honoured for the sake of his regal fiery seat. What follows seems to infer the latter: if so, then "Respect to your great place!" is spoken with a tone of contempt, such as implies a strong negative.

> Thus to retort your manifest appeal,
> And put your trial in the villain's mouth
> Which here you come to accuse.

LUCIO. This is the rascal; this is he I spoke of.

ESCALUS. Why, thou unreverend and unhallow'd friar,
> Is't not enough thou hast suborn'd these women
> T' accuse this worthy man, but, in foul mouth,
> And in the witness of his proper ear,
> To call him villain? and then to glance from him
> To th' Duke himself, to tax him with injustice?—
> Take him hence; to th' rack with him!—We'll touse[257] you
> Joint by joint, but we will know his purpose.
> What! unjust?

DUKE. Be not so hot; the Duke
> Dare no more stretch this finger of mine than he
> Dare rack his own; his subject am I not,
> Nor here provincial.[258] My business in this state
> Made me a looker-on here in Vienna,
> Where I have seen corruption boil and bubble
> Till it o'errun the stew;[259] laws for all faults,
> But faults so countenanced that the strong statutes
> Stand like the forfeits in a barber's shop,
> As much in mock as mark.[260]

---

[257] To *touse* is to *pull, pluck,* or *tear to pieces.* Kindred in sense, and probably in origin, to *tease*; used of carding wool.—In "joint by joint," the first *joint* is a dissyllable; as often *fire, hour,* &c., and sometimes *hear, year,* &c.

[258] Not subject to the ecclesiastical authorities of this *province.* The word was thus applied to a given circuit of spiritual jurisdiction.

[259] A *stew*, as the word is here used, is, properly, a brothel or house of prostitution. And there is a comparison implied between such a house and a cauldron, like that of the Weird Sisters in *Macbeth*, in which the hell-broth or devil-soup of corruption bubbles and foams, till the cauldron *boils over,* and floods the surroundings.

[260] Barbers' shops were much resorted to as places for lounging and loafing. To keep some sort of order, and perhaps to promote drinking, (for barbers often kept drinks on sale,) a list of petty *fines* or *forfeits* was hung up for such and such disorders. These forfeits would naturally cause more mirth than fear, or be more *mocked* than *marked,* inasmuch as the barbers had no power to enforce them, and the incurring of them was apt to occasion sport.—Kenrick, in his review of Johnson's *Shakespeare,* gave sundry specimens of these forfeits from memory, as he claimed to have seen them in a barber's shop in Yorkshire. I subjoin two of them:

> Who checks the barber in his tale
> Must pay for each his pot of ale.

> And he who can, or will, not pay,
> Shall hence be sent half-trimm'd away;
> And, will-he, nill-he, if in fault,
> He forfeit must, in meal or malt.

ESCALUS. Slander to the state!—Away with him to prison!

ANGELO. What can you vouch against him, Signior Lucio? Is this the man that you did tell us of?

LUCIO. 'Tis he, my lord.—Come hither, good-man bald-pate. Do you know me?

DUKE. I remember you, sir, by the sound of your voice. I met you at the prison, in the absence of the Duke.

LUCIO. O did you so? And do you remember what you said of the Duke?

DUKE. Most notedly, sir.

LUCIO. Do you so, sir? And was the Duke a fleshmonger, a fool, and a coward, as you then reported him to be?

DUKE. You must, sir, change persons with me ere you make that my report: you, indeed, spoke so of him; and much more, much worse.

LUCIO. O thou damnable fellow! Did not I pluck thee by the nose for thy speeches?

DUKE. I protest I love the Duke as I love myself.

ANGELO. Hark how the villain would gloze[261] now, after his treasonable abuses!

ESCALUS. Such a fellow is not to be talked withal. Away with him to prison!—Where is the Provost?—Away with him to prison! Lay bolts enough upon him: let him speak no more.—Away with those giglets[262] too, and with the other confederate companion!

[*The* PROVOST *lays hands on the* DUKE.]

DUKE. Stay, sir; stay awhile.

ANGELO. What! resists he?—Help him, Lucio.

LUCIO. Come, sir; come, sir! come, sir; foh, sir! Why, you bald-pated lying rascal! you must be hooded, must you? Show your knave's visage, with a pox to you! show your sheep-biting[263] face, and be hanged an hour![264] Will't not off? [*Pulls off the friar's-hood and discovers the* DUKE.]

DUKE. Thou art the first knave that e'er made a Duke.—

First, Provost, let me bail these gentle three.—

[*To* LUCIO.] Sneak not away, sir; for the friar and you

---

[261] To *gloze*, or to *gloss*, is, properly, to *explain*, hence to *gloss over*, *palliate*, or *explain away*: here it carries the further sense of to *cajole*, to *flatter*, or to *fawn. Glossary* is from the same root.

[262] *Giglets* or *giglots* is *jades* or *wantons.* So in Cole's *Dictionary*: "A Giglet, *fœmina petulans.*" Also in Cotgrave: "A Giggle or Gigglet, *Gadrouillette.*"—"Gadrouillette, a *minx, giggle, flirt, callet.*"

[263] *Sheep-biting* is an old term of abuse or reproach, probably meaning *slanderous, censorious,* or *back-biting.*

[264] "Be hang'd an hour," and "be curst awhile," were petty imprecations; *an hour* and *awhile* being mainly expletive.

Must have a word anon:—Lay hold on him.

LUCIO. This may prove worse than hanging.

DUKE. [*To* ESCALUS.] What you have spoke I pardon; sit you
>   down.—
>   We'll borrow place of him.—[*To* ANGELO.] Sir, by your leave.
>   Hast thou or word, or wit, or impudence,
>   That yet can do thee office?[265] If thou hast,
>   Rely upon it till my tale be heard,
>   And hold no longer out.

ANGELO. O my dread lord,
>   I should be guiltier than my guiltiness,
>   To think I can be undiscernible,
>   When I perceive your grace, like power divine,
>   Hath look'd upon my passes.[266] Then, good Prince,
>   No longer session hold upon my shame,
>   But let my trial be mine own confession:[267]
>   Immediate sentence then, and sequent death,
>   Is all the grace I beg.

DUKE. Come hither, Mariana.—
>   Say, wast thou e'er contracted to this woman?

ANGELO. I was, my lord.

DUKE. Go, take her hence and marry her instantly.
>   Do you the office, friar; which consummate,[268]
>   Return him here again.—Go with him, Provost.

[*Exeunt* ANGELO, MARIANA, *Friar* PETER, *and* PROVOST.]

ESCALUS. My lord, I am more amazed at his dishonour
>   Than at the strangeness of it.[269]

DUKE. Come hither, Isabel:
>   Your friar is now your prince. As I was then
>   Advertising[270] and holy to your business,

---

[265] That is, *serve thy cause,* or do thee *service. Office* in the Latin sense. The Poet has it repeatedly so. Also the verb to *office.*

[266] *Passes* is probably put for *trespasses;* though sometimes explained *artful devices, deceitful contrivances,* and *courses.* Shakespeare has, I think, no other like instance of the word. Perhaps we should take it as meaning, simply, "what I have done," or "the things of my past."

[267] That is, "let my own confession give me up to punishment without a trial." The Poet has many similar inversions.

[268] Which (the marriage) *being consummated.* The Poet has many such shortened preterites; as *situate, consecrate, suffocate,* &c.

[269] The meaning seems to be, "the strangeness of his dishonour is not, to me, the most amazing part of it"; alluding, perhaps, to the stranger methods by which Angelo's exposure has been effected.

Not changing heart with habit, I am still
Attorney'd at your service.
ISABELLA. O, give me pardon,
That I, your vassal, have employ'd and pain'd
Your unknown sovereignty.
DUKE. You are pardon'd, Isabel.
And now, dear maid, be you as free to us.
Your brother's death, I know, sits at your heart;
And you may marvel why I obscur'd myself,
Labouring to save his life, and would not rather
Make rash remonstrance[271] of my hidden power
Than let him so be lost. O most kind maid,
It was the swift celerity of his death,
Which I did think with slower foot came on,
That brain'd[272] my purpose. But peace be with him!
That life is better life, past fearing death,
Than that which lives to fear: make it your comfort,
So happy is your brother.
ISABELLA.I do, my lord.

[*Re-enter* ANGELO, MARIANA, *Friar* PETER, *and the* PROVOST.]

DUKE. For this new-married man approaching here,
Whose salt[273] imagination yet hath wrong'd
Your well-defended Honour, you must pardon
For Mariana's sake: but as he adjudg'd your brother,—
Being criminal, in double violation
Of sacred chastity and of promise-breach,
Thereon dependent, for your brother's life,[274]—

---

[270] *Advertising* here means, no doubt, *instructing at counselling*; much the same as *attorney'd*, second line after. A like use of the word occurs in the first scene of this play: "I do bend my speech to one that can my part in him *advertise.*" See page 20, note 9.

[271] *Remonstrance* for *demonstration*, *display*, or *exhibition*; a common usage of the Poet's time. So in Hooker, iii. 7, 8: "Heresy prevaileth only by a counterfeit show of reason; whereby notwithstanding it becometh invincible, unless it be convicted of fraud by manifest *remonstrance* clearly true and unable to be withstood."

[272] To *brain* for to *kill* or to *knock out the brains*. So in *The Tempest*, iii. 2: "Then thou mayst *brain* him." And in *I Henry IV.*, ii. 3: "Zounds, an I were now by this rascal, I could *brain* him with his lady's fan."

[273] *Salt*, here, is *lustful* or *lecherous*. So in *Othello*, ii. 1: "For the better compassing of his *salt* and most hidden-loose affection." Also in *Timon of Athens*, iv. 3: "Make use of thy *salt* hours: season the slaves for tubs."

[274] The language is somewhat obscure. The meaning is, "in breaking the promise of pardon to your brother, which promise was conditioned or made dependent upon his violation of your honour." "Being criminal *in double*" means "being *doubly* criminal in." Many like inversions.

The very mercy of the law cries out
Most audible, even from his proper tongue,[275]
An Angelo for Claudio, death for death.
Haste still pays haste, and leisure answers leisure;
Like doth quit like, and measure still for measure.
Then, Angelo, thy fault's thus manifested,—
Which, though thou wouldst[276] deny, denies thee vantage:
We do condemn thee to the very block
Where Claudio stoop'd to death, and with like haste.—
Away with him.

MARIANA.O my most gracious lord,
I hope you will not mock me with a husband!

DUKE. It is your husband mock'd you with a husband.
Consenting to the safeguard of your Honour,
I thought your marriage fit; else imputation,
For that he knew you, might reproach your life,
And choke your good to come: for his possessions,
Although by confiscation they are ours,
We do instate and widow you withal
To buy you a better husband.

MARIANA. O my dear lord,
I crave no other, nor no better man.

DUKE. Never crave him; we are definitive.

MARIANA. Gentle my liege—[*Kneeling.*]

DUKE. You do but lose your labour.—
Away with him to death!—[*To* LUCIO.] Now, sir, to you.

MARIANA. O my good lord!—Sweet Isabel, take my part;
Lend me your knees, and all my life to come
I'll lend you all my life to do you service.

DUKE. Against all sense you do importune her.
Should she kneel down in mercy of this fact,
Her brother's ghost his paved bed would break,
And take her hence in horror.

MARIANA. Isabel,
Sweet Isabel, do yet but kneel by me;
Hold up your hands, say nothing,—I'll speak all.
They say, best men moulded out of faults;
And, for the most, become much more the better
For being a little bad:[277] so may my husband.

---

[275] That is, the language of his *own* mouth, or the utterance of his *own* tongue. *Proper* used in its right classical sense. So before in this scene: "And in the witness of his *proper* ear." The Poet has many instances of such use.

[276] *Wouldst* for *shouldst*. The auxiliaries *could*, *should*, and *would* were continually used as equivalents in the Poet's time.—*Quit*, second line before, is *requite*, *repay*, or *return*. Shakespeare often has it so.

O Isabel, will you not lend a knee?
DUKE. He dies for Claudio's death.
ISABELLA. [*Kneeling.*] Most bounteous sir,
    Look, if it please you, on this man condemn'd,
    As if my brother liv'd: I partly think
    A due sincerity govern'd his deeds
    Till he did look on me; since it is so,
    Let him not die. My brother had but justice,
    In that he did the thing for which he died:
    For Angelo,
    His act did not o'ertake his bad intent,
    And must be buried but as an intent
    That perish'd by the way:[278] thoughts are no subjects;
    Intents but merely thoughts.
MARIANA. Merely, my lord.
DUKE. Your suit's unprofitable; stand up, I say.—
    I have bethought me of another fault.—
    Provost, how came it Claudio was beheaded
    At an unusual hour?
PROVOST. It was commanded so.
DUKE. Had you a special warrant for the deed?
PROVOST. No, my good lord; it was by private message.
DUKE. For which I do discharge you of your office:
    Give up your keys.
PROVOST. Pardon me, noble lord:
    I thought it was a fault, but knew it not;
    Yet did repent me, after more advice:[279]
    For testimony whereof, one in the prison,
    That should by private order else have died,
    I have reserved alive.
DUKE. What's he?
PROVOST. His name is Barnardine.

---

[277] On the principle, perhaps, that Nature or Providence often uses men's vices to scourge down their pride. So in *All's Well*, iv. 3: "Our virtues would be proud, if our faults whipp'd them not." Hooker has a like thought in one of his sermons: "What is virtue but a medicine, and vice but a wound? Yet we have so often deeply wounded ourselves with medicines, that God hath been fain to make wounds medicinal; to cure by vice where virtue hath stricken. I am not afraid to affirm it boldly, with St. Augustine, that men puffed up through a proud opinion of their own sanctity and holiness, receive a benefit at the hands of God, and are assisted with His grace, when with His grace they are not assisted, but permitted, and that grievously, to transgress; whereby, as they were in over-great liking of themselves supplanted, so the dislike of that which did supplant them may establish them afterwards the surer."

[278] Like the traveller who dies on his journey, is obscurely buried by strangers, and is thought of no more.

[279] "After more advice" is on *further consideration.* The Poet uses *advice* repeatedly in this way.

DUKE. I would thou hadst done so by Claudio.
    Go fetch him hither; let me look upon him.

    [*Exit* PROVOST.]

ESCALUS. I am sorry one so learned and so wise
    As you, Lord Angelo, have still appear'd,
    Should slip so grossly, both in the heat of blood
    And lack of temper'd judgment afterward.
ANGELO. I am sorry that such sorrow I procure:
    And so deep sticks it in my penitent heart
    That I crave death more willingly than mercy;
    'Tis my deserving, and I do entreat it.

    [*Re-enter* PROVOST, *with* BARNARDINE, CLAUDIO *muffled, and* JULIET.]

DUKE. Which is that Barnardine?
PROVOST. This, my lord.
DUKE. There was a friar told me of this man:—
    Sirrah, thou art said to have a stubborn soul,
    That apprehends no further than this world,
    And squar'st thy life according. Thou'rt condemn'd;
    But, for those earthly faults, I quit them all;[280]
    And pray thee take this mercy to provide
    For better times to come:—Friar, advise him;
    I leave him to your hand.—What muffled fellow's that?
PROVOST. This is another prisoner that I sav'd,
    Who should have died when Claudio lost his head;
    As like almost to Claudio as himself. [*Unmuffles* CLAUDIO.]
DUKE. [*To* ISABELLA.] If he be like your brother, for his sake
    Is he pardon'd; and for your lovely sake,
    Give me your hand and say you will be mine;
    He is my brother too: but fitter time for that.
    By this Lord Angelo perceives he's safe;
    Methinks I see a quick'ning in his eye.—
    Well, Angelo, your evil quits[281] you well:
    Look that you love your wife; her worth worth yours![282]—
    I find an apt remission[283] in myself;

---

[280] *Quit*, here, is *acquit*, that is, *release* or *discharge*; a frequent usage.

[281] Here, again, *quits* is *requites* or *revenges*. See page 100, note 276.

[282] Meaning, apparently, "May her virtue *call forth, kindle*, or *develop* an answering virtue in you!"

[283] "Apt remission" probably means *aptness* or inclination to *remit* offences; that is, to pardon them.

And yet here's one in place I cannot pardon.—
[*To* LUCIO.] You, sirrah, that knew me for a fool, a coward,
One all of luxury, an ass, a madman;
Wherein have I so deserved of you
That you extol me thus?

LUCIO. Faith, my lord, I spoke it but according to the trick.[284] If you will hang me for it, you may; but I had rather it would please you I might be whipped.

DUKE. Whipp'd first, sir, and hang'd after.—
Proclaim it, Provost, round about the city,
If any woman wrong'd by this lewd fellow,—
As I have heard him swear himself there's one
Whom he begot with child,—let her appear,
And he shall marry her: the nuptial finish'd,
Let him be whipp'd and hang'd.

LUCIO. I beseech your highness, do not marry me to a whore! Your highness said even now I made you a Duke; good my lord, do not recompense me in making me a cuckold.

DUKE. Upon mine Honour, thou shalt marry her.
Thy slanders I forgive; and therewithal
Remit thy other forfeits.—Take him to prison;
And see our pleasure herein executed.

LUCIO. Marrying a punk, my lord, is pressing to death, whipping, and hanging.

DUKE. Slandering a prince deserves it.—

[*Exeunt* OFFICERS *with* LUCIO.]

She, Claudio, that you wrong'd, look you restore.—
Joy to you, Mariana!—Love her, Angelo;
I have confess'd her, and I know her virtue.—
Thanks, good friend Escalus, for thy much goodness
There's more behind that is more gratulate.[285]—
Thanks, Provost, for thy care and secrecy;
We shall employ thee in a worthier place.—
Forgive him, Angelo, that brought you home
The head of Ragozine for Claudio's:
The offence pardons itself.—Dear Isabel,
I have a motion much imports your good;
Whereto if you'll a willing ear incline,
What's mine is yours, and what is yours is mine:—
So, bring us to our palace; where we'll show

---

[284] "After my custom, in the way of jest or course of sport."
[285] More to be rejoiced at, or more worthy of gratulation.

What's yet behind that's meet you all should know. [*Exeunt.*]

THE END

Made in United States
North Haven, CT
28 February 2022

16619974R00064